What Shall
We Do
With Love?

What Shall We Do With Love?

by

Ernest Eberhard, Jr.

BOOKCRAFT, INC.
SALT LAKE CITY, UTAH

Litho in U.S.A.
by

FOREWORD

No subject is more popular than dating, courtship, and marriage. The interest of a young man and woman in each other is the heart and core of much music, drama, and literature. It is forever stealing the center of the stage and lingers through all of life's acts.

The relationship of young men and women to each other leads to happiness or misery and determines these ends more potently than money, position, or fame. Yet these relationships are often entered into without guidance or thought. The most important steps in life are all too often taken with the least preparation and prevision of the purposes and goals to be achieved.

In this book the author has provided for youth, and for those who counsel youth, a simple analysis of the problem "What shall we do with love?" He has outlined a detailed course which will make the journey of life interesting and purposeful and which will help young people avoid the pitfalls.

The author weaves into his treatment of this vital subject the spiritual factors so stressed by the Master. He brings into sharp focus the great and eternal rewards promised to those who make their marriage a true partnership with God.

This book is the result of more than a quarter of a century of counseling with teenagers, and reflects the richness of that experience.

WILLIAM E. BERRETT

ACKNOWLEDGMENTS

This book is an attempt to achieve a complete frame of reference on one of youth's most perplexing problems— "What shall we do with love?" It represents a more or less continued effort for over twenty years, and is designed to be positive and appealing to young people and still be fully oriented to the principles of the Restored Gospel.

I acknowledge my indebtedness to many hundreds of seminary students and their teachers who have voluntarily evaluated this project as it developed over the years.

I express deep appreciation to Elder Delbert L. Stapley of the Council of the Twelve and President Marion D. Hanks of the First Council of the Seventy for the stimulation they gave to write something worthwhile on this subject which is so vital to the welfare of our youth, and to President A. Theodore Tuttle, presently of the First Council of the Seventy, and formerly General Supervisor of Seminaries and Institutes, for his constant encouragement to proceed with this work.

I also express deep appreciation to President William E. Berrett, Vice Administrator in charge of Institutes and Seminaries, and Boyd K. Packer, General Supervisor for the Department of Education, for their encouragement and helpful comments, and to members of the Church Reading Committee for their suggestions and changes.

Many persons, too numerous to mention individually, have assisted in the preparation of this book. I am grateful to Marba C. Josephson, Associate Editor of *The Improvement Era,* and Rita S. Robinson, Editorial Assistant of Bookcraft, for their help in editing the manuscript, and to Marvin W. Wallin of Bookcraft for his personal interest and assistance. I appreciate the excellent illustrations by Richard Scopes.

Above all, I express my appreciation to my wife, Nevon, for her faith which through the years has helped me bring this project to a successful conclusion.

ERNEST EBERHARD, JR.

CONTENTS

CONTENTS— *(Continued)*

Part One

Marriage and Parenthood —
A Partnership With God,
the Eternal Father

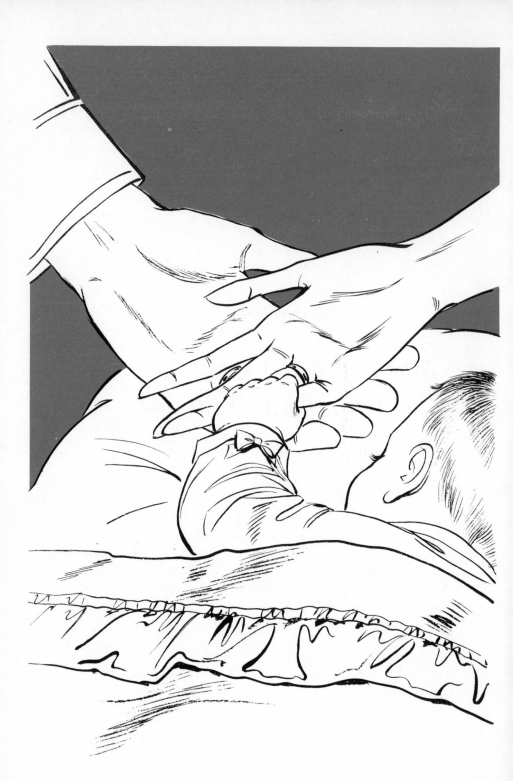

Partnership with God

CHAPTER ONE

FOR TIME AND ETERNITY

A feeling of peace filled Temple Square. The early morning air was delightfully invigorating. Dew still sparkled on the grass and flowers. Birds sang joyously in the trees.

A young guide, surrounded by a group of tourists, had reached the monuments of the Prophet and his brother Hyrum. Sensing that they were not going to be led through the Temple one young lady raised her hand.

"Why can't we go through the Temple?" she asked.

"Because it has been dedicated for special, holy purposes and only members of the Church who are worthy are allowed to enter."

"What do you do in there?" asked a man in front. "Meditate?"

"Well, I am sure many of those who enter do meditate while there. But that isn't the real purpose of our temples. We have temples so we can have a place to perform certain sacred ordinances. For instance, suppose a young couple wants to get married. If they are truly converted Latter-day Saints they will not be satisfied with a marriage with a built-in divorce."

"A built-in divorce? I have never heard of such a foolish thing in all my life!" retorted an elderly lady. "And I have attended many Church weddings during my life," she added.

"That is because you haven't thought through the full meaning of the ceremony your minister uses," replied the guide. "Do you remember ever hearing him say, 'until death do you part'?"

"Why . . . yes, he always says it," admitted the lady, "but I have never thought much about it. Are you trying to say you believe God will take that statement seriously? He is a just and loving God. Surely he would never separate a couple who have lived and worked together through thick and thin for fifty years?"

"Well," rejoined the guide, "it isn't what God wants; it's what we, his children, want. Do you believe God forces man to act in a certain way?"

"Oh no. I firmly believe in the personal responsibility of man. I believe he is responsible for his own decisions and acts."

"What, then, can God do if people are satisfied with a ceremony which specifies separation at death? Let us go back to the beginning of this matter. What was the first recorded marriage?"

"I would say it was that of Adam and Eve."

"Who performed it, and in what condition were Adam and Eve when it was performed?"

"The Bible says God gave Eve to Adam as a helpmate, and they were immortal at the time. I guess that made their marriage immortal too," replied the elderly matron.

"That is right," replied the guide.

"Well," replied the lady, "I am going back home and really talk to my minister. I don't want to feel I will be separated from my departed husband."

After the tour was over and the guide had dismissed the group, a half dozen tourists indicated that they had a few more questions to ask.

"We were wondering," said one man who seemed to be a spokesman for the group, "if your Church has other ideas about life which Christian Churches do not have. It seems to me I heard someone say you believe in a sort of pre-existence. Is that true?"

"It certainly is. Latter-day Saints do not believe eternity begins when one dies. They believe it is a continuum divided into three different segments called pre-existence, mortality and immortality. We believe we had a spiritual father and mother and that life began for each of us with a spiritual creation in the spirit world or pre-existence. There, after a period of progress, growth came to a halt. We could go no further until our spirit bodies had been clothed with a physical body. Jesus, our Savior, accepted a plan which, if we too follow it, will make possible our eternal exaltation. In this life we are to choose between good and evil and learn obedience to the laws of joy and progress. One of the greatest joys in this life comes to us when we become co-creators with our Heavenly Father by providing bodies and loving homes for those spirits who are yet awaiting their opportunity to work out their exaltation.

"It is in the temple that this plan is put into operation by sacred vows and covenants the bride and groom take upon themselves. When they join their hands across the altar in the temple and are married by a man holding the keys of the sealing power, their love will be raised to a height never known by those who are married only until death do you part.'"

"What about the children born to the couple," asked a young woman, "will they be part of the family circle?"

"Oh yes," replied the guide, "we say all their children will be born 'under the covenant' and will be part of the family circle in the eternities."

"From what you say it looks as if you want to link all your ancestors into one great family," stated one intent listener.

"That is right. God is our Father. We are his children. Life is for the purpose of helping us to be worthy to live with him and to be formally joined as a family. Do you have a family, Sir?"

"Yes. We do. My lovely wife and I have five wonderful children."

"Would you like to live together throughout eternity in love and companionship as you do now?"

"There is nothing we desire more. But this is so new! So different! It is our first acquaintance with such a wonderful doctrine! Strange—I have a sense of joy—a feeling that life has a meaning I had always hoped for but never known until now. Could we find out more?"

"You surely can!" replied the guide. "Give me your name and address and we will have the missionaries in your area call on you after your return home."

"Thank you," said the man, handing the guide his card.

With a radiant look on his face, he turned to his wife. "Mary, this past hour may well be the turning point in our whole lives."

"It surely will," she said, "if we can make our marriage and family secure for time and eternity."

CHAPTER TWO

WHAT REASONS DO PEOPLE OF THE WORLD
HAVE FOR GETTING MARRIED?

People of the world get married for love (as they understand it), for financial security, social prestige, companionship, or because of some common interest such as music, art, or sports. Many people who love and desire children marry to have a family even though they do not understand pre-existence and exaltation as members of the Church do.

However, some teenagers have still other reasons for getting married. Since this study is designed to highlight the problems of you, who are between the ages of 12 and 20, let us consider the thinking of young people of your age.

Teenage marriages have increased to an astonishing extent in the last few years. A national magazine recently reported that the divorce rate among these early marriages is as much as three times higher than among those waiting until the age of twenty.

Since so many teenage marriages end in failure, you young people who have any regard for your own happiness will want to be wary of using any of the following reasons for marrying early:

1. **Some teenagers are extremely romantic.** They are often completely unrealistic when they fall in love. They fall in love with love! This "early love" was designed to be a self-starter of the budding emotional life, but young

people tend to mistake the self-starter for the engine that carries us on to mature love.

One psychologist said, "Everything is like a story-book to them. They believe people marry and automatically live happily ever after."

A social worker stated it a little differently, "They have a vague dream of living in an idyllic, pastel-walled apartment and giving each other breakfast in bed simultaneously for the rest of their lives."

2. **Immature teenagers feel that the mere act of getting married makes them adults.** Adulthood seems to have so many advantages. Many young people want these as quickly as possible. They do not want to pay for them. They do not worry about earning them. They do not realize that the advantages of true adulthood must be earned to be real and lasting. Marriage seems a quick, pleasant, sure way of getting the privileges of adulthood, of being allowed to come and go and do as they please. Some teenagers actually resort to early marriage to have an excuse for quitting school.

3. **Teenagers who go steady early and persistently push themselves to a point where they can no longer control themselves.** This has led many teenagers to be indiscreet. As a result they must marry in order to give their unborn children a name.

4. **Teenagers desire to imitate others.** Nothing is more important to them than to be accepted by their peer group. Just stop and think of the number of fads which have been current during your high school career — socks up, socks down, tight skirts, bulky sweaters, jeans, hot rods,

jive. You complete the list. As a result of this desire to be one with the group, some teenagers have even started "marriage epidemics"!

School authorities have observed in some instances that if a couple of boys who are prominent in school athletics or are popular in other activities get married, a rash of marriages and engagements breaks out. Some teenagers are not so rash. They merely acquire a "steady" or sport a dime-store diamond that has no real significance but serves to identify them with the group.

5. **Some teenagers want to escape a bad home environment.** Perhaps the home is stricken with real poverty where physical conditions are on a bare subsistence level. Perhaps the father drinks and beats and abuses the wife and children. Perhaps the mother drinks and neglects the home and children. In severe cases it may be that both parents drink. It may be that there is no love in the home, and that the children are not wanted. From such home environment teenagers feel they simply must escape. Marriage seems a quick, pleasant, sure way out, more often for girls than for boys. When this is the case, girls can be talked into some of the most unfortunate, heartbreaking relationships in existence. Because, they hope for so much, they can be deceived so easily.

6. **Parents openly or secretly want the children out of the way.** They may be waiting for them to grow up so they can get a divorce. Perhaps they want to move to another locality, and the children do not. The mother possibly wants to go to work again. In some instances the parents do not want to support their children any longer and urge them to get on their own.

7. **Some very young people marry impulsively.** It may be the result of a dare. Perhaps a crowd of young folks, far from home, start challenging each other to get married. Perhaps a pair of teenagers is with an older couple who are eloping, so they are taunted into getting married too.

These impulse marriages are often triggered by the use of alcohol which has deadened good judgment.

Marrying on the "rebound" is common among young people of unstable emotional temperament who cannot stand to be disappointed, crossed, or defeated in life. When they are turned down by one person to whom they are really attracted, they marry someone else for sheer spite.

8. **Young people marry sometimes to spite their parents.** It may be the parents are unreasonably strict or do not really love their children but do not want them to do anything to hurt the family name. The children feel they can get square with their parents by getting married — to the utter dismay and shock of their elders. Thus young people feel they have an effective way to "pay back" their parents for the real or fancied wrongs they feel have been inflicted upon them.

9. **Young people are misled by what may be called counterfeits of love.** These might be the opportunity for living one's life with a "divine" dancer, the school beauty queen, an athletic hero, the outstanding school thespian around whom a Hollywood aura has been spun in the minds of the members of the opposite sex. These personality traits seem all important to teens. It never occurs to them that in a few years these characteristics will not be in existence, will be totally unimportant in the new scheme

of things, or forgotten by those who speak of them so often now.

10.   **The stress seems to be on sense satisfaction from early life in our present culture.** The relative wealth of people enables them to buy rich foods, drinks, fine clothes, entertainment, automobiles, etc., as they please. People are not willing to carry on activities for their own entertainment but try to get it by watching movies and TV, or by reading trash. Young people who have grown up on a diet of sense satisfaction feel no need to restrain themselves in the least when they mature biologically and feel the pull of the powers of procreation.

On the other hand they may come from good homes and have been properly taught to live clean moral lives. They do not want to commit any sin, so they simply get married as young as possible in order to get an opportunity to indulge legally in this new and overwhelming area of sensual experience.

11.   **Many young people have never been taught the true purposes of life.** They have no goals for the development of their personalities and characters. They do not understand their important roles as co-creators with God. They do not understand the need to prepare themselves for these supreme roles. This lack of purpose spills over into other areas. Some teenagers actually quit school in order to get married and "live" as they put it.

As this study progresses you will be interested in evaluating for yourself how these reasons, which are so forceful in the lives of so many young people in the world, fit into the true scheme of life in its entirety as revealed by a good understanding of the gospel.

CHAPTER THREE

WHAT IS GOD'S PLAN FOR YOUR MARRIAGE?

Some sociologists and anthropologists, who have the limited perspective of intelligent, scientifically trained human beings, express the belief that marriage in its different forms is a human institution created by different cultures to maintain an orderly working form of society. However, Latter-day Saints know that this is not so. They know that marriage is part of an eternal plan designed to elevate man to Godhood. They know that they are literal, spiritual children of God, and can achieve an exaltation comparable to God's own.

When Was Marriage Instituted?

Marriage was anticipated at the time of your spiritual creation by your Heavenly Parents when you were created male and female. In the Doctrine and Covenants we read: (1) "And that he created man, male and female, after his own image and in his own likeness, created he them; . . ." (D & C 20:18.)

God's reason for doing this is indicated in the Bible: (2) "So God created man in his own image, in the image of God created he him, male and female created he them.

"And God blessed them, and God said unto them, Be fruitful, and multiply, and replenish the earth, and subdue it. . . ." (Genesis 1:27-28.)

This scripture indicates that each of you was intended to fill a definite role, one which neither man nor woman could fill alone. Truly "man is not without the woman, neither is the woman without the man in the Lord."

Biologists tell us that the existence of mothers and fathers makes it possible for each individual to be born into the world with a personality and character which will never be duplicated. Some scientists claim that a single pair of parents would have to give birth to as many as 250,000,000 children before any two would be exactly alike. Thus physical heredity, plus the experience you had in pre-earth life, plus the influence of your earthly stay make it certain that in all eternity there will never be another you. Only through the miracle of birth can each spirit child of God receive a body with its marvelous possibilities, and be set on the way to exaltation. Since you have been given this unique body and personality which will last you throughout the eternities, should you not examine carefully God's plan for you? No other plan can guide you to a fullness of joy.

Life

"I'm going to send you down to Earth,"
    Said God to me one day.
I'm giving you what men call birth,
    To-night, you'll start away.
I want you there to live with men,
    Until I call you back again."

I trembled as I heard him speak,
    Yet knew that I must go.
I felt his hand upon my cheek
    And wished that I might know
Just what on earth would be my task,
    And timidly I dared to ask.

"Tell me before I start away
    What thou wouldst have me do,
What message wouldst thou have me say,
    When shall my work be through
That I may serve thee on the earth
    Tell me the purpose of my birth."

God smiled at me and softly said,
    "Oh, you shall find your task.
I want you free life's paths to tread,
    So do not stay to ask.
Remember, if your best you do,
    That I shall ask no more of you."

How often as my work I do,
    So commonplace and grim,
I sit and sigh and wish I knew
    If I am pleasing him.
I wonder if with every test,
    I've truly tried to do my best.

—Anon.

Who Performed the First Marriage?

To set the pattern, God himself performed the first marriage, that of our ancestral parents, Adam and Eve. He gave them definite instructions as to the purpose and activities of their union as you can read in Genesis. It is very important to remember that this marriage was performed before Adam and Eve became mortal, and therefore death would not alter its course in the future. It was intended to be permanent or eternal.

While Jesus, the Only Begotten of the Father, was performing his ministry on earth, the Pharisees tried to trap him into admitting that God did not have a definite, permanent form of marriage, when they attempted to get him to sanction the institution of divorce. Let us follow the conversation as recorded in Matthew:

> The Pharisees also came unto him, tempting him, and saying unto him, Is it lawful for a man to put away his wife for every cause?
>
> And he answered and said unto him, Have ye not read, that he which made them at the beginning made them male and female,
>
> And said, For this cause shall a man leave father and mother, and shall cleave to his wife: and they twain shall be one flesh?
>
> Wherefore they are no more twain, but one flesh. What therefor God hath joined together, let no man put asunder.
>
> They say unto him, Why did Moses then command to give a writing of divorcement, and to put her away?
>
> He saith unto them, Moses because of the hardness of your hearts suffered you to put away your wives: *but from the beginning it was not so.* (Matthew 19:3-8.)

The last line indicates that men even in the days of Moses had strayed from the attitude toward marriage which God the Father had in mind when he created our spirits.

Marriage is so important that the Lord saw fit to give a revelation on the necessity of entering into the marriage covenant. This is what he said:

> And again, verily I say unto you, that whoso forbiddeth to marry is not ordained of God, for marriage is ordained of God unto man.

Wherefore, it is lawful that he should have one wife, and they twain shall be one flesh, and all this that the earth might answer the end of its creation; . . . (D & C 49:15-16.)

Will you please read that last line again? How could marriage be any more important? It is a supreme ordinance. Our world was created that marriage and all it implies could be realized. Without it the creation of the earth would have been without purpose.

What Do Our Modern Prophets Say About the Purpose of Marriage?

Your entire future life throughout eternity depends on the nature of your marriage. Joseph Smith explained it thus:

"Except a man and his wife enter into an everlasting covenant and be married for eternity, while in this probation by the power and authority of the Holy Priesthood, they will cease to increase when they die; . . ." (May 15, 1843) (*Times and Seasons* 4:194.)

President Wilford W. Woodruff has this to say: "It is our duty to get married at the proper time. It is the law of God." (M.S. 51:595-1889.)

President Joseph F. Smith was speaking to young men in the following quotation, but we may be sure he was also aware of the importance of marriage to young women.

I want the young men of Zion to realize this institution of marriage is not a man-made institution. It is of God. It is honorable, and no man of marriageable age is living his religion who remains single. It is not simply devised for the convenience alone of man, to suit his own notions, and his own ideas to marry and then divorce, to adopt and then to discard, just as he pleases. There are great consequences connected with it, consequences which reach beyond this present time into all eternity, for thereby souls are begotten into the world, and men and women obtain their being into the world. Marriage is the preserver of the human race. Without it the purposes of God would be frustrated; virtue would be destroyed to give place to vice and corruption, and the earth would be void and empty. (Joseph F. Smith. *Gospel Doctrine*, pp. 272-273.)

Finally we have the testimony of our living prophet, the beloved President of the Church, David O. McKay.

Truly no higher ideal regarding marriage can be cherished by young people than to look upon it as a divine institution. In the minds of the young such a standard is a protection to them in courtship, an ever-present influence inducing them to refrain from doing anything which may prevent their going to the temple to have their love completed in an enduring and eternal union. It will lead them to seek divine guidance in the selecting of their companions, upon the wise choice of whom their life's happiness here and hereafter is largely dependent. "Our home joys," says Pestolozzi, "are the most delightful earth affords, and the joy of parents in their children is the most holy joy of humanity." It makes their hearts pure and good; it lifts them up to their Father in heaven. Such joys are within the reach of most men and women if high ideals of marriage and home are properly fostered and cherished.

And yet, if I mistake not the signs of the times, the sacredness of the marriage covenant is dangerously threatened. There are too many thoughtless, hasty marriages entered into without enough time to consider the consequences. (David O. McKay, *Gospel Ideals*, p. 462.)

How May the Nature and Purpose of Marriage Be Best Summarized?

1.   Marriage is an institution which was planned at the time of our spiritual creation by God the Father.

2.   It is only through the proper use of the power of procreation, that a fulness of joy and exaltation can be realized.

3.   In marriage and parenthood, as God designed it to be, we come closer to being like our Creator in power and achievement than in anything else we do. The importance of parenthood was eternally fixed when the Savior told his disciples they should address their Creator and God in prayer with the words "Our *Father*, which art in heaven."

4.   Had there been no provision for marriage and the placing of immortal spirits in earthly tabernacles, the whole universe would have been void and without purpose.

5.   Without provision for a continuation of the family circle and relationships, any plans which human beings may have for a future life after death will be lacking in the activities and purposes which bring meaning to life. Think of the sorrowful emptiness of life throughout the eternities for those who can no longer enjoy the blessings of marriage and children! Only those marriages will endure which are sealed by the proper authorities in the Temples of the Lord.

President Joseph Fielding Smith explains this rather fully in the following quotation.

PROCREATION LIMITED TO CELESTIAL BODIES. *Some will gain celestial bodies with all the powers of exaltation and eternal increase.*

Those who enter the terrestrial kingdom will have terrestrial bodies, they will not shine like the sun, but will be more glorious than those who receive the telestial glory. . . .

Those who receive the exaltation in the celestial kingdom will have the "continuation of seeds forever." *They will live in the family relationship.* In the terrestrial and in the telestial kingdoms there will be no marriage. Those who enter there will remain "separately and singly" forever.

Some of the functions in the celestial body will not appear in the terrestrial body, neither in the telestial body, *and the power of procreation will be removed.* I take it that men and women will, in these kingdoms, be just what the so-called Christian world expects us all to be — neither man nor woman, merely immortal beings having received the resurrection. (Joseph Fielding Smith. *Doctrines of Salvation,* pp. 287-288.)

6.   No career, no invention, no achievement is as great as that of rearing a child and placing it firmly on the road to eternal exaltation. All the mortal works of man will pass away except those which further the purpose and plans of our Heavenly Father. Thus the achievements of successful parents have no foreseeable limit, because their children, being potential gods, have no limits set to their growth, power, and glory.

7.   It is not enough to become physical parents of these spirits. We must also have the capacity and desire to nourish them spiritually. We must lead them along a path of love and loyalty to God. We must train them to apply the gospel until they can guide themselves. We must do all we can to help them make sure their exaltation.

8.   Our ancestral parents, Adam and Eve, were

chosen to be the first man and woman to enter into this eternal partnership of marriage with each other and thus become partners with God the Father in bringing about the immortality and eternal life of man.

They began the task of providing bodies and opportunities for exaltation for those who were to be privileged to live on the earth. Now, each of you, as you grow to maturity, will have to decide whether you would like to enter into a like partnership. You will have to decide whether you want to achieve a fullness of love under God's plan, or whether you want to accept a makeshift union which men of the world have arranged. This will be the most important decision you will make as a Latter-day Saint during your sojourn on this earth. This decision will never cease to affect your life throughout eternity. How important it is for you to think clearly and select wisely!

Part Two

What Is Love?

CHAPTER FOUR

LOVE AND ITS COUNTERFEITS

Have you ever tried writing a definition of love? Was it difficult? Did you feel like doing as one boy did who tried and tried and finally ended up writing *yah* on his paper? You do not need to be discouraged. There are few words which have as much and as many meanings behind them as the word *love*. Let's look at the way various people understand love.

What kind of love made God offer up his Only Begotten Son? What was the love which caused Jesus to go to Jerusalem of his own free will to be crucified that the bonds of death might be broken for us? Where does the love come from which makes a man like Dr. Albert Schweitzer give his life to the natives of Africa? What do parents feel who still show love toward their children even when these children have terribly disappointed and disgraced them?

On the negative side we might ask why a man who steals his neighbor's wife, or a woman who steals her friend's husband, gives love as an excuse. Young men sometimes call on girls to "prove" their love in a way which will bring only shame and sorrow. What is this love they talk about? Is it related to the love couples experience who kneel at the altar and covenant with the Lord? Can physical indulgence compare in any way to the wondrous love experienced by those who know that their union is blessed and sanctified by their Creator? Can physical love compare

to the complete love of those who know they are sealed
together for time and eternity? Yet all these people, in these
various situations, speak of their emotions with the same
word — LOVE.

What do you think of the following description?

No one knows whence it comes, all that anyone
can possibly know is that it has come. You are going
down the street, pondering the future of the League of
Nations, you turn a corner, or step into an elevator, or
an automobile crashes in your front yard. Your psy-
chological moment steps out and looks you in the eye,
and then it is on. A moment ago it was not on, now
it is; that is all there is to it. That is all you will ever
know about it.

Love is a mysterious visitation. It comes out of
the nowhere into the here, unexpected, unannounced,
perhaps uninvited. It is unpredictable, uncontrollable,
undependable. (*Modern Marriage*, Paul Popenoe.)

Is this the kind of love some people feel as they fall
in and out of love about as regularly as the new moon ap-
pears in the heavens?

What about the "romantic" or "true" love you read
about so much and hope to experience yourselves? Why
does it seem to pass some people by? Why does such love
last for some people and disappear so quickly for others?
Whence does it come? Can we understand it so it can be
made to serve us in our lives?

For some answers to these questions let us turn to life
itself and see whether it can give a clue as to the nature and
quality of the maturing love you will need for a happy and
successful marriage.

Is There a Pattern for the Development of Love?

Professional people, people who have applied the yardstick of systematic study and observation to a study and observation of love say there is a definite, persistent pattern in its development. In fact, they say it can be fairly well diagrammed, as the chart on next page indicates.

Before we go any farther, it is recommended that you study the chart rather thoroughly. Can you pick up the trail of the development of your own ability to be interested in others, to want to help them, to work with them, in other words, to love them? Perhaps it would be well to go back beyond earth life and pick it up at the beginning point for us all.

How Is the LDS Idea of Love More Complete and Satisfying Than That of the World?

This question is stated as if this were a fact which does not need to be proved. As members of the Church of Jesus Christ we believe this is true.

Let us examine the gospel concept and see why this is so. We know that in the pre-existence we loved God and our Elder Brother Jesus Christ more than we loved Satan. We were among those who fought against Satan and his hosts who had rejected God's plan of salvation. After this struggle we progressed in our obedience and love of God as far as it was possible to do so in the spirit world. We had subdued the spiritual element and made it our servant. But there was another category of element, the earth, flesh and matter, in its gross form, with which we had had no experience. To have this opportunity for further

The Development of the Power to Love

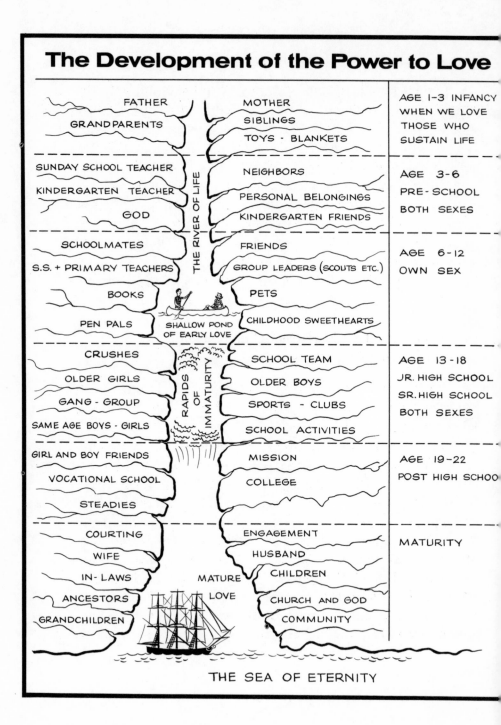

FATHER	MOTHER	AGE 1-3 INFANCY
GRANDPARENTS	SIBLINGS	WHEN WE LOVE
	TOYS - BLANKETS	THOSE WHO
		SUSTAIN LIFE
SUNDAY SCHOOL TEACHER	NEIGHBORS	AGE 3-6
KINDERGARTEN TEACHER	PERSONAL BELONGINGS	PRE-SCHOOL
GOD	KINDERGARTEN FRIENDS	BOTH SEXES
SCHOOLMATES	FRIENDS	AGE 6-12
S.S. + PRIMARY TEACHERS	GROUP LEADERS (SCOUTS ETC.)	OWN SEX
BOOKS	PETS	
PEN PALS	CHILDHOOD SWEETHEARTS	

THE RIVER OF LIFE

SHALLOW POND OF EARLY LOVE

CRUSHES	SCHOOL TEAM	AGE 13-18
OLDER GIRLS	OLDER BOYS	JR. HIGH SCHOOL
GANG - GROUP	SPORTS - CLUBS	SR. HIGH SCHOOL
SAME AGE BOYS - GIRLS	SCHOOL ACTIVITIES	BOTH SEXES

RAPIDS OF IMMATURITY

GIRL AND BOY FRIENDS	MISSION	AGE 19-22
VOCATIONAL SCHOOL	COLLEGE	POST HIGH SCHOO
STEADIES		
COURTING	ENGAGEMENT	MATURITY
WIFE	HUSBAND	
IN-LAWS	CHILDREN	
ANCESTORS	CHURCH AND GOD	
GRANDCHILDREN	COMMUNITY	

MATURE LOVE

THE SEA OF ETERNITY

growth we needed to come to this sphere through birth to earthly parents.

When we arrive here, we are without any habits, ideas, or set patterns of response. This condition is an evidence that our belief, "As man now is God once was, and as God now is man may be. . .," is literally true. Our future is un-limited and unfettered' by instincts. We can go as far as our faith, obedience, and power to love will take us.

A baby's first response to the world is entirely physical. If there is a baby in your home, you will certainly know what this means. People say that all babies do is eat and sleep — or cry. Yes, they do cry if they are cold, hungry, colicky, or have any physical distress of any kind. They do not care whether it is day or night, whether the parents are awake or asleep, whether they are sick, tired, or busy.

Gradually this condition changes. Baby brother learns to recognize his mother's voice, the feel of her hands, her body, and her touch. Whereas only food or attention to his physical needs quieted baby before, now this is not enough. He smiles and coos happily when his mother approaches, plays, or talks with him.

Baby brother's spirit is beginning to assert itself, and love of another kind is sending forth its tender shoots. This love is probably still quite selfish. Baby loves mother be-cause of what she does for him. But even so we like to be-lieve the light of love is breaking through the barriers of the physical element.

When mother brings baby food or starts to pick him up, listen to his delighted gurgling.

If baby brother does not experience these first ap-proaches to love, if he feels rejected and neglected in babyhood, he may never be able to love others adequately. He may grow up to be withdrawn, fearful, and insecure. He may want to reach out in maturing love to others, but always draws back from any outgoing contact with them when the time comes to do so.

Our ability to love and be loved is predicated upon the number of contacts we make with the outside world, the nature of these contacts, and how we perceive or evaluate them. This evaluation of our contacts with others must undergo a steady and definite growth as we mature.

If some of these streams of influence fail to enter our lifestream, it will never have a full flow. The channel of our emotional life will remain shallow, full of treacherous sandbars and shoals. On the other hand if some streams are full of evil influences, hate, and fear, they are like poison and contaminate and discolor the whole emotional stream of our lives.

If we feel accepted, loved, and cherished as we progress in life, we develop the ability to be outgoing and to love others. If we feel rejected and unloved, we tend to reject, to become hostile, to fight for the things and stations we want in life. The fact that we cannot get them this way is immaterial; we still try.

What Is the Relationship Between Emotional and Spiritual Maturity and the Ability to Love?

People are becoming emotionally and spiritually mature when they change from a "me" orientation toward life and their fellow men to a "we" orientation — from a receiving to a giving attitude, from a desire to be served and favored, to serving and helping others. Sometimes this condition is "faked," and people indicate their actions are motivated by love when they are not. These are counterfeits of love, and since they are sometimes highly camouflaged, it might be well to examine some of them in order that they may not lead astray later in life.

What Are Some Counterfeits of Love?

Counterfeits of love are all characterized by the giving of a little in an attempt to receive much in order to satisfy one's own desires, ambitions, or wants.

It may sound terribly romantic for a boy to say to a girl, "I can't live without you." Some girls are taken in by this false protestation of love. However, if you will examine it a little more closely, you will see it is an infantile form of affection. True love gives — gives equal measure and more. False love wants, takes, satisfies itself at the expense of another. The boy who says, "I can't live without you," is thinking only of himself, his own feelings, his own wants. Basically he may be as infantile emotionally as a child who cries no matter how it disturbs the parents.

One of the most devilish, vicious counterfeits of love is all too often encountered by girls who are asked by a boy to prove their love by submitting to an immoral proposal. This counterfeit is such a common occurrence and is so satanic and destructive that all young people should be warned concerning it.

Its true nature is revealed when it is realized that the boy offers nothing and demands in return almost everything worthwhile in life, except life itself. Hitler had an axiom. He said people will believe a lie more readily if it is as far from truth as it can be. Such is this lie about love. It is so tremendous some girls are led to believe it, and yet it is an almost perfect example of what love is not.

There is another imitation which is quite deceiving. It is based on our desire to feel successful and important. Sometimes a member of the opposite sex can supply one with items which increase one's sense of social worth and standing. Such an item may be wealth which for many holds a promise of a fulness of life. Often it's a beautiful convertible which causes the heads of all the other girls to turn in envy. It may be the boy is so handsome that the girl feels life would be a complete success if only she had such an escort. It may be that his athletic prowess has made him the school idol. She wants to bask in this reflected glory, so she falls in love with his popularity. A boy might feel a girl's beauty is so desirous that he could love her forever just because of this favored condition of form and feature. A boy who is timid and shy might meet a girl who is over-confident and aggressive. In her presence he feels protected and safe and no longer feels the need of developing his own manhood. Loving a person because he has these qualities is to accept a counterfeit.

Still another of the most deceiving and common counterfeits is the acceptance of the idea that the excitement which young people experience when they first associate together is an evidence of true love. That it may be an evidence of the strong attraction maturing women and men feel for each other cannot be denied. To assume that this feeling of excitement is evidence of the ability and maturity necessary to carry through the obligations of marriage and parenthood is another matter. Psychologists and marriage counselors commonly speak of it as "falling in love with love." Some young people marry on the basis of this phy-sical attraction rather than waiting to find a mate with whom they can find complete love and happiness.

What Happens to Marriages Based on Counterfeits of Love?

The divorce rate of those marrying at a very early age is seven to eight times as high as it is for those who marry later. This indicates that this feeling of excitement is an undeveloped and incomplete facet of human feeling and emotion which needs time and experience for its frui-tion. To feel excited and highly attracted to a member of the opposite sex is one thing. To be attracted to a young man or woman because he or she has the qualifications to help one fulfill his destiny in life is quite another. There should be an element of attraction, of personal liking, of love, in both situations. However, quite often, that is *all* there is in "early love." The result is that when it has ful-filled its particular role, as the beginning form of love, it seldom sustains the next phase, and therefore it dies. "Early love" has the same function in the development of mature love as does the self-starter in an automobile. The self-starter is only intended to apply the initial power so the engine can be started and supply greater and more perman-ent power. "Early love" is the beginning impulse, which puts into motion the growth of all the faculties, personality traits, and strength of character which result in the mature power to love God, our families, and all mankind. It may have great possibilities as does a tiny seedling which may someday be a mighty oak, but the embryo oak needs water and other favorable conditions to achieve its full majestic stature. "Early love" is a promising seedling, but it needs protection and preparation through education, experience in living with and for others, and the development of one's personality before it can stand the rigors of marriage and family responsibility.

There are no doubt many other counterfeits of love. It will be to your advantage to be on the lookout for them, and safeguard yourself against them. You can easily detect them with this yardstick: they all want; they take; they do not give; they do not help; they do not serve.

How Does Satan Measure Love?

It might be well to remember that Satan practises more deceptions in this area of the attraction of a man and a woman to each other than in almost any other field. Since he and his cohorts will forever be denied bodies and the power to create and through love to develop joy in the lives of their own offspring, they create endless counterfeits to block the progress and joy of men.

Satan and his hosts would like to make it impossible for you to gain a celestial body. Satan acts like the lobster. If you put two lobsters on a flat plate and go away they will be there when you get back. This is so because the minute one lobster tries to crawl off, the other will grab him and pull him back. Likewise, the devil will keep you on the plate with him, at his level, as tenaciously as the lobster. To achieve his goal he uses many approaches. He began with our ancestral parents, Adam and Eve. He hoped to thwart the purposes of mortality by leading them into temptation. Satan knows that if he can confuse you as to the proper use of your manly and womanly powers he is about as close to reducing you to his status as he can get.

He constantly counterfeits, misrepresents and distorts the purposes and possibilities God gave you as young men and women. Some of these counterfeits are so close to the genuine article that only through the discerning power of the Holy Ghost will you be able to detect them. Those who are not deeply imbued with the desire to build the kingdom of God and be obedient to the gospel plan will have a most difficult time eluding his grasp in this day and age. Faithful members of the Church have less need to worry. They are largely beyond the grasp of his destructive power.

Of all the sons and daughters of God, Satan was the most selfish. He wanted all the glory for saving man. This selfishness he strives to build in us. He stresses physical attraction, excitement, and temporary goals with every imaginable device available. He never places a price tag on his wares when he offers them for sale. It is so high and horrible that he would be without customers if he put price tags on his merchandise. What a price will be paid by those who follow him!

They will inherit a lesser kingdom unless they fully and speedily repent. They will be denied the privilege of having their families in eternity. They will be denied the power to beget spirit children. They will be servants to those who have earned a higher glory. They will never fully enjoy the fruits of their own labors. Their energies and talents will be spent building up someone else's kingdom. They will never experience a fulness of joy.

Try to imagine what that would mean to you! Could you imagine a more terrible fate? There will be little growth or expansion of the power to love and receive love. On the other hand, if you adhere to the gospel plan fully and faithfully, this outgoing, expanding, joyful emotion will become greater and greater until it envelopes all phases of your life. You will be bathed in the warmth and glory of love eternally.

In order that you may visualize both conditions try to remember how wonderful you feel when you find love and acceptance and devotion from your family and friends. Contrast this feeling with your emotion and frustration during hours of rejection, fear, jealousy, or hate.

God's way is the path of love in increasing measure. Satan's way is hate, in the same degree. You are faced with making increasingly important choices between types of conduct and ways of living which will lead you either toward the expanding exaltation of love or toward the restricting chasm of selfishness.

CHAPTER FIVE
WHAT MAKES LOVE GROW?

From our study in chapter one, we have seen that love is a growing, dynamic, expanding emotion. It has been said that inexperienced people feel that falling in love, being in love, and loving are expressions of the same emotion. Actually this is not so. Only "mature love" is closely related to the ultimate basic emotion all men seek, called joy.

We are told in the Book of Mormon that ". . . men are, that they might have joy." Joy is the reward of loving service. We may experience joy in this life as brothers or sisters, as children of a family, as friends, as members of activity groups, and as participants in school. Tomorrow we may experience joy as wives or husbands, as fathers or mothers, as grandfathers or grandmothers. Some may experience joy as missionaries to the world; others as researchers in genealogy, or as Temple workers. Some may have joy through service as bishops or stake presidents, or in similar positions of leadership, or greater ones. Who knows, one of you may receive joy through the high calling of a General Authority. You girls will have countless opportunities for joy through service in the Sunday School, Primary, Mutual, or Relief Society.

Thus it can be seen that the gospel plan provides for an ever-widening measure of joy through service. When we pass into eternity and are resurrected, our ability to experience joy will be multiplied many fold.

Joy and the ability to love and be loved can in many respects be regarded as synonymous. The ability to experience and express love consistently and fully must be based on service to God and our fellowmen. Beginning love, early love is incomplete because it is based on self-interest rather than interest in others.

How Should We Regard "Early Love"?

Most psychologists agree that "early love" is contrectative — that is, it is based on the sensations derived from physical touch. At this time, because of a lack of experience, personality development, and general maturity, the spiritual touch is largely non-existent.

The physical touch produces a thrill which can never be more than temporary unless it is combined with a spiritual purpose. This does not mean that physical sensations are bad or are to be denied entirely. They have a God-given purpose at the right time and place. The trouble comes when this timing and purpose are perverted and used for selfish and unworthy purposes alone. Trying to achieve permanent love by physical sensation alone is like trying to force the maturing of a beautiful flower by forcing the petals apart with the fingers. A beautiful blossom must unfold slowly, naturally, by the achievement of the growth pattern in the plant. The development of the power to love by human beings is not much different. It is the result of the maturity of a complicated inner life process whose full nature is known only to our Father in heaven. However, we do know something of the process of this maturation. Of this we shall speak more in detail later.

To experience love continually requires the ability to grow into each successive phase of life in a fully mature fashion. The important thing to note is that these phases

Is it OK to be in love as a teenager?

I t's certainly *possible* and *natural* for teenagers to be in love—their feelings, though perhaps less mature, are no less real than the feelings of people who are older. But as Latter-day Saint youth, you need to consider romantic love in the context of God's plan and the covenants you have made with Him.

Though you *are* doing things now to prepare for marriage, it's still a ways off, so wondering whether you're in love with someone is a bit premature. Both you and the other person have more learning and growing to do as well as some important decisions to make before focusing on being in love. Finding someone to be in love with is best left for the courtship phase of life, which nowadays generally comes after secondary school, a mission (for young men), and the beginning of higher education or career training. For now, in the dating stage of life, follow the counsel of prophets: have fun and don't let things get serious (see *For the Strength of Youth* [2011], 4–5). **NE** decided to follow the *For the Strength of Youth* standards and not date until I was 16. For me, it didn't feel right to kiss at my age either, so I didn't feel comfortable with the scenes. I asked my director about it, and she said we'd just cut the kiss off before it happened.

I was relieved but felt bad because the lead male thought I just didn't want to kiss him. I tried to explain my decision, but he thought I was making excuses. I didn't know what to do to make him believe me, but then my friends assured him that I was telling the truth. Since they aren't members of the Church, I was surprised at how much they'd noticed and supported my standards.

As we continued practicing for our show, I saw others around me standing up for my beliefs. When I wanted to find a modest dance costume, many girls helped me find one that worked; when I had to be dragged around on stage, the actor holding my feet made sure my skirt always covered my knees; and when we had to learn extra dances, we sacrificed lunch hours practicing then instead of on Sundays.

Some people still questioned my actions, but I hadn't realized until then that an influence I'd been. By simply living the gospel, I was being an example, and others had noticed and were willing to stand by me to help me continue keeping my standards.

I know that Heavenly Father is always looking out for us and will give us ways to share the gospel in our lives every day—even by simply setting an example.

Samantha W., Alberta, Canada

become increasingly less physical and more spiritual. This is in keeping with the gospel plan of life. Unless it were so the spirit would not be gaining control over gross matter o which it becomes temporarily subject at birth.

The scripture says, "God is spirit, and those who worship him must worship him in spirit and in truth." This does not mean that God is without a body but rather that the joy, eternal life, and exaltation he enjoys are the results of spiritual growth, power, and control. The love based on physical experience serves only as an initiator or self-starter for spiritual growth and development.

Jesus said unto him, Thou shalt love the Lord thy God with all thy heart, and with all thy soul, and with all thy mind.

This is the first and great commandment.

And the second is like unto it, Thou shalt love thy neighbour as thyself.

On these two commandments hang all the law and the prophets. (Italics mine. Matt. 22:37-40.)

Notice the last line — all the law and the prophets hang on our ability to love God and our fellow men. If we love these two, we will find our love strong enough and permanent enough to carry us successfully through all phases of dating, courting, marriage, and rearing a family. Without a love-orientation of life we run a great risk of becoming a member of that horde of unhappy and frustrated human beings who have felt that physical love was enough, only to have this love end in the anger, hate, and sorrow of separation or divorce. We should not be satisfied with the level of true love we have attained today. Rather, we should regard it as a basis for growth of an even greater love tomorrow.

CHAPTER SIX

WHAT ARE THE CHARACTERISTICS OF "MATURE LOVE"?

As has been indicated before, there is a point of development in human life when the ability to love matures to the point where marriage may be properly contemplated. The questions are, what is the nature of this maturity, how can we know whether we have achieved it, and are we ready for a partnership in marriage?

Sometimes poets have an insight into human life and emotion which partakes of the nature of the divine. Such an insight is expressed by Sir Walter Scott in the following verse:

> True love's the gift which God has given
> To man alone beneath heaven.
> It is not fantasy's hot fire,
> Whose wishes soon as granted fly.
> It liveth not in fierce desire. . . .
> With dead desire, it doth not die.
> It is the secret sympathy,
> The silver link, the silken tie,
> Which heart to heart and mind to mind
> In body and soul can bind.
>
> (Familiar Quotations "Lay of the Minstrel,"
> Sir Walter Scott.)

Let us ponder the thoughts of this poetic analysis and put them into expressions of your everyday lives. You will then have a usable yardstick for determining the maturity of your own lives.

First, love is not animalistic in nature. It is an attraction with which God has imbued only his children. There is a great element of spirituality in it. One desires to build the personality and life of one's mate. A determination is present to further God's eternal plan to bring the highest possible exaltation to all his children. There is a strong element of future planning in it. True love looks to something beyond today, tomorrow, or even beyond mortal life. Psychologists would say it has a strong element of consciousness in it, an awareness that you are a person who has a destiny unlike that of any other of God's creations.

Second, it has permanency. It is not extinguished by physical expression and satisfaction. Its value does not lie in the expression of mere passion. Its expression is tied to an increased feeling of tenderness, care, and loyalty in many other aspects of life which have nothing to do with pure sense satisfaction.

Third, it is an expression of ourselves which is of an involved nature. It ties together many aspects of our lives — the way we feel in our hearts, the way we think in our minds, the way we sense physically, and finally a combination of all of these in a full expression of our soul's unified desire.

In its mature state love is a complex emotion. Probably the most complex which human beings experience. Not only is it complex, but it is also delicate. It cannot be hurried, forced, or demanded. True love can be obtained from others only on the basis of free-agency. It is present in many activities of life — in our religious, vocational, cultural, social, and recreational lives. It gives color, purpose, and a delightful quality of zest and enjoyment to all life's activities.

By contrast we find that "early love" may operate almost solely in our social and recreational lives and may leave the other areas untouched.

Man possesses a mind, an intelligence which craves satisfaction the same as the body does. Therefore the expression of love on a physical basis alone — no matter how enticing and glamorous movies and novels make it — does not yield a permanent, maximum satisfaction to human beings. When people satisfy only their physical desires, with no thought of the spiritual phase, they soon feel a strong, gnawing sense of dissatisfaction.

People who marry solely on the basis of a strong physical attraction for each other, soon find something lacking in their marriage. Because they do not understand the nature of mature love, the necessity for spiritual purpose and companionship in their relationship, they assume their trouble stems from the fact that they have married the wrong person. Often they seek a divorce so that they can marry this "right" person. But since they are still looking for the wrong thing in love, they are usually disappointed. After entering into several such marriages, they may give up and live in bitterness and frustration. Others actually may become lost in gross immorality as they try to wring intellectual and spiritual satisfaction from physical satisfaction.

How Must "Mature Love" Be a Partnership?

"Mature love" is a voluntary partnership. It is a partnership of equality, based not on the superiority of the man over the woman, but on a differentiation of their God-given functions in life. If the man may be called the head of the family, certainly the woman is the heart.

In our own lives, we must have a head, and a heart. We do not say one is more vital than the other. They both make a unique contribution. The man who is all brain, all intellect and no feeling is not a well-rounded individual. Neither is the man or woman who is all emotion.

The gospel gives us an opportunity to express this in our lives. The father holds the priesthood. He is responsible to serve with love, devotion and humility. He may receive inspiration to guide his family on its earthly journey. But without a worthy helpmeet, a faithful daughter of God who will walk with him through mortal life and on into eternity, he cannot receive a fulness of life and exaltation. On this the Lord has been most clear.

> And again, verily I say unto you, if a man marry a wife, and make a covenant with her for time and all eternity, if that covenant is not by me or by my word, which is my love, and is not sealed by the Holy Spirit of promise, through him whom I have anointed and appointed unto this power, then it is not valid neither of force, when they are out of the world, because they are not joined by me, saith the Lord, neither by my word; when they are out of the world it cannot be received there, because the angels and gods are appointed there, by whom they cannot pass; they cannot therefore, inherit my glory for my house is a house of order, saith the Lord God. (D & C 132:18.)

Although the mother does not formally hold the priesthood and exercise its powers it can function fully in the husband's and father's life only with her.

"Early love" is a perfectly normal, stage-development phase of mature love. When it has properly served its purpose it has laid the foundations for the next phase. There is an "early love" phase of marriage which also passes in a year or two after the honeymoon. This must be replaced by a phase which is centered primarily in God and his purposes rather than in a continuation of the "for each other" interest which brought them together.

President Brigham Young puts it even more strongly:

> But the whole subject of the marriage relation is not in my reach, nor in any other man's reach on this earth. It is without beginning of days or end of years, it is a hard matter to reach. We can tell some things with regard to it; it lays the foundations for worlds, angels, and for Gods; for intelligent beings to be crowned with glory, immortality and eternal lives. In fact, it is the thread which runs from the beginning to the end of the holy Gospel of Salvation . . . of the Gospel of the Son of God; it is from eternity to eternity! (*Discourses of Brigham Young*, p. 302.)

A recent writer, a physician of international note, although not a member of the Church, adds the testimony of his great experience in the following quotation.

> When it is not only the husband and wife who say Yes to each other, but God says His great Yes to their marriage, then within their marriage things become possible which would be impossible without it. (*Love, Skill and Mystery*, Theodore Bonet, Doubleday & Co. Inc., Garden City, N.Y., 1958, p. 181.)

In some matters the marriage partners will have individual differences which will actually give interest and vitality to their marriage. There can be variation in taste for food, clothing, and recreation. Hówever, in certain matters of thinking, feeling, and believing they should be as one if their love is to live and flourish.

The couple should be united in their ultimate goal in life for themselves and their children. Their moral values should be the same. They should not only have the same basic religious faith but also a high degree of interest and activity in the Church. There are members of the Church living in less harmony with the principles of the gospel than people who are not members. Care should be taken that the similarity in faith is real and not just imagined.

The writer has always given the following counsel to young people who have come to him for recommends during the ten years he was the bishop of a large ward:

> Your love for each other will grow in the same measure as you both cultivate and express your love for your Heavenly Father through service to Him and your fellow-men.

The testimony of those who put this advice to the test was always that it was truly so. The writer has never found a star to guide the ship of matrimony on the sea of life which was so unchanging and unfailing as this observation. Think about it deeply. Will you accept the challenge to try it?

Part Three

What Do We Need
For a Successful Marriage?

CHAPTER SEVEN

HOW PERMANENT IS "HONEYMOON LOVE"?

If you were a judge in a domestic relations court, you would probably hear the following story told over and over. Yes, there would be some variations, but they would not be too important.

Let's listen as a sobbing, heartbroken girl, whom we shall call Mary, tells of her marriage to a young man named Jack. He stands beside her before the judge, shifting uneasily from one foot to another. Sometimes he bristles up and then again slumps down as he looks at his wife in bewilderment and dismay, probably wondering how his feelings toward her could change so completely in such a short time. Here is Mary's story.

"We were 'head over heels in love' when we married. Of that there was no doubt in anyone's mind. We both felt as if we were floating on a cloud of love. People said, 'It is the finest match we have ever seen,' and, 'what a perfect marriage,' or 'have you ever seen a couple so happy?'

"And yet in two years our dream is finished. We have hit the earth with a terrible, jarring thud. It all happened without a lot of warning. We started to disagree more and more. We got on each other's nerves terribly. It got so we went out of our way to spite each other. Now I hate him. I want him out of my sight. I don't love him at all. We've tried to patch things up, but they only come apart a little more."

Jack added a few bitter words of his own. Careful questioning by the judge showed they had nothing left in the way of love for each other. There was no point of contact in their lives. With a sigh the judge gave the order to dissolve their marriage—one more in the endless parade of broken marriages which shuffled through his court each day. Mary and Jack left—another couple in the unending train of baffled, heartbroken, disillusioned couples.

A little notice in the paper the next day stated the divorce was granted for "mental cruelty." This could mean almost anything. It might have meant more had it been called mismatching. Yet, two years before, this marriage had been called a perfect match.

It is hard to believe that love doesn't go on of its own accord. But divorce court statistics, which tell the truth without favor, indicate love needs more than a start. It needs regular and sufficient nourishment if it is to remain a living, growing emotion. Yes, it is a sad truth that the stirred-up emotional state people sometimes feel during courtship may gradually dwindle away after marriage.

When God placed the emotion of love in the human breast, he gave it the power to make people blind to the little defects all mortals have. Sometimes it adds glamor where there is none. In olden times people associated this temporary response with witchcraft and even consulted certain people who were supposed to have a recipe for a magic brew of love. This bit of emotional witchcraft is probably necessary in our lives. Lovers rarely marry real people. They generally see their lovers through the halo of an ideal, or wrapped in a long-cherished dream.

After marriage there is a change. People stop dreaming. Gradually their feet settle on the ground. Reason, sanity, the light of day return. Then there must be something else to take the place of this delightful blindness, this substitution of an ideal or dream for reality.

On What Is a Successful Marriage Based?

All of you who have due regard for your happiness and welfare in the years ahead will want to know the answer to the above question. There is no simple answer. A successful marriage is the result of many skills, achievements, and personality—characteristics which young people must have acquired in the years before their marriage. It would no doubt be hard to name and discuss all of them. Then, too, it would be hard to say how much of one or another is necessary for a happy marriage. Also, since personality and character traits are not found in the same amount or combination in any two persons, it would be difficult to list them in the order of their importance. If it were possible to know which are the most important, or what lies hidden in the human soul, marriage could be reduced to a stable and standardized formula. Since human beings are complex, this cannot be done. We must be satisfied with a partial understanding, which is, however, very important and helpful.

There follows a discussion of seven fields of living. An attempt will be made to relate them to one another and your final goal—a happy and successful marriage.

They will be treated in the following order:

1. Religion
2. Character
3. Age
4. Personality
5. Heredity
6. Health
7. Recreational interests.

CHAPTER EIGHT

HOW IMPORTANT IS IT TO MARRY A MEMBER OF THE CHURCH?

Have you ever asked yourself the above question? Since many Latter-day Saint families have moved to other parts of the United States or the world, and many non-members have come to live among us here in the center stakes of Zion, the problem has become more pressing and frequent. In areas where members of the Church are in a great minority, the number of "part-member marriages" has increased tremendously.

The problem of marrying outside of one's faith is not a new one. The Bible tells us it was present thousands of years ago:

> And Abraham said unto his eldest servant . . . thou shalt not take a wife unto my son of the daughters of the Canaanites, among whom I dwell:
>
> But thou shalt go unto my country, and to my kindred, and take a wife unto my son Isaac.
>
> (Gen. 24:2-4.)

> And Isaac called Jacob, and blessed him, and charged him, and said unto him, Thou shalt not take a wife of the daughters of Canaan.
>
> Arise, go to Padanaram, to the house of Bethuel thy mother's father; and take thee a wife from thence of the daughters of Laban thy mother's brother.
>
> And God Almighty bless thee, and make thee fruitful, and multiply thee, that thou mayest be a multitude of people.
>
> (Gen. 28:1-3.)

Jacob heeded his father's counsel and became father of the covenant people. Most of us are descended from his faithful son Joseph who was sold into Egypt.

When the Lord brought the children of Israel (Jacob's descendants) out of Egypt, he commanded that they should not marry unbelievers, lest they be led to idolatry and the worship of false Gods:

> Neither shalt thou make marriages with them; thy daughter thou shalt not give unto his son, nor his daughter shalt thou take unto thy son.
>
> For they will turn away thy son from following me, that they may serve other gods: so will the anger of the Lord be kindled against you, and destroy thee suddenly.
>
> (Deut. 7:3-4.)

Early-day Saints were counseled against marrying outside of the Church because of the galling burden they would have to bear:

> Be ye not unequally yoked together with un- believers; for what fellowship hath righteousness with unrighteousness? and what communion hath light with darkness?
>
> 2 Cor. 6:14.)

Modern prophets have repeated this ancient warning. In the early days of the Church, President Brigham Young warned the mothers to teach their daughters to marry in the Church, and that if they did not, they surely would lose their exaltation.

President Joseph F. Smith offered the advice:

> That believer and unbeliever should not be yoked together, for sooner or later, in time *or in eternity* (italics mine), they must be divided again. I would like to see Latter-day Saint women marry Latter-day Saint men . . . Let Methodists marry Methodists;

Catholics marry Catholics; Presbyterians marry Presbyterians; and so on to the limit. (*Gospel Doctrine,*
Joseph F. Smith, p. 279.)

The late Apostle John A. Widtsoe who made a
thorough study of this problem made this plea,

> You of Israel, marry within the Church. Human
> experience and safe counsel are clearly against "mixed
> marriages." The countless cases on record are full
> evidence that more joy is realized, more usefulness
> attained when persons of the same faith marry.

Even among Protestants where matters of creed and
dogma are often not so important, there seems to be serious
doubt concerning the advisability of people marrying members of different faiths.

When studies are made of the results of mixed marriages, the results show a rather uniform pattern.

In 1938, a study was made among some 12,000 young
people in the State of Maryland. These young men and
women, ages 16-24, were asked what the religious affiliations of each of their parents were and also whether their
father and mother were living together, were separated,
or divorced.

The findings were as follows:

Religious Affiliation of Parents	Percentages of Homes Broken by Divorce, Desertion or Separation
None	16.7
Both Jewish	4.6
Both Catholic	6.4
Both Protestant	6.8
Mixed	15.2

Here is a definite, statistical answer to the question at the beginning of this chapter. When people marry outside their own church, the divorce rate is two or three times higher than if they marry members of their own faith. It is also interesting to note that the divorce rate is highest among those who do not belong to any church.

The *Harvard Survey of Happy Families,* a recent study, involving 60,000 American families, also bears this out. Reported under the caption of "The facts about interfaith marriages" this is the report:

Nine thousand of the 60,000 families studied in the *Harvard Survey* had mixed marriages. The two researchers sought neither to denounce nor defend interfaith marriages but simply to discover the facts about them. They found:

1. Couples with different religious affiliations have fewer children than those who marry within their own faith.

2. Children of interfaith marriage are much less likely to finish high school than those whose parents are of the same religious faith.

3. Six out of every ten children of a Catholic-Protestant marriage end by rejecting all religions —Catholic, Protestant, and others.

4. About half of the Catholic men who marry non-Catholics abandon their faith.

5. Men and women of all faiths showed a higher divorce rate when they married someone of a different religion. In an interfaith marriage by a Protestant, the divorce rate was two or three times as great as in all-Protestant marriage. Among Catholics, who marry out of their church, the increase was three or four times. Among Jews, who marry non-Jews, five or six times.

6.   The teenage arrest rates are much higher in mixed marriage families. When Protestant men married outside their faith in St. Louis, Omaha, and Denver, their youngsters suffered twice as many arrests as youngsters in single-faith homes. In marriages between Catholics and non-Catholics the arrests of teenage children in every city doubled or tripled. The children of Jewish husbands and Gentile wives in Boston, St. Louis, Denver, and Omaha had four to ten times as many arrests for juvenile offenses as the children of all-Jewish marriages in those cities.

7.   . . . if a person without religion marries a person without any religion, divorce, desertion, delinquency are generally shown in the *Harvard Survey of Happy Families* to quadruple. But if the person without any religion engages in a "mixed marriage," that is, if he marries someone with some religious adherence, his socially negative record is cut from a quadruple threat to a mitigated double threat. His wife is even an economic asset, for when men without religious commitment marry women who belong to a church or synagogue there is a significant percentage more who will earn over $5,000.00 a year than if they had married women, who, as themselves, have no religious connection. This striking pattern of the social advantage of religious membership was found in every city studied. (*This Week Magazine*, Sept. 20, 1959.)

In addition to the above evidence we have the experience of our returned missionaries who can all tell many stories of the heart-rending visits they have made to the unhappy homes of those who have married outside the Church.

Some of you will immediately say that you know some LDS who have married non-members and have brought them into the Church. You may also point out that there are wonderful people who live very righteously in most respects, who are not LDS.

These points must be quickly and fully conceded. But the chances for the success of such a marriage are so low and the risk of failure so high that to base one's choice on the chance of being an exception seems foolhardy. How often would you take a chance on a business proposition if you knew the odds were eight to one against you? There are those who have made a study of this matter who feel these are about the odds that must be faced. Under certain definite situations these odds might be lowered. What these conditions are will be discussed in a later chapter.

Why Do Part-Member Marriages Result in So Many Marriage Failures?

There are no doubt many reasons why part-member marriages fail. It will be possible to consider only a limited number.

For the first, let us go back to Sir Walter Scott's poetic definition of love, wherein he says it is:

> The silver link, the silken tie,
>
> Which heart to heart and mind to mind,
>
> In body and soul can bind.

Although other factors, such as personality enter in, this silken tie seems to be basically the most important factor in a successful marriage. It is made up in a large part of what the Church can do for you if you will serve it faith-

". . . too many basic differences . . ."

fully. These services may not seem important during court-ship and early marriage but when the real issues of life have to be met, the part-member couple soon realizes how deep and how vital a true religious faith is.

Sometimes couples try to work out compromises by not going to any church, or only to his church or her church. All too often they learn by bitter experience that this is not possible. Families do not seem to be able to divide their allegiance and participate in organizations which have different creeds and beliefs. These differences affect the emotional and spiritual well-being of individual family members too much. They either become lukewarm and stop going to any church, or one spouse forces the other through argument or will power to join his or her church. Religion, instead of being an area of agreement, harmony, and strength in marriage, becomes a shattering, disorganiz-ing influence. Instead of fostering greater mutual love and respect, such a difference in religion breeds distrust, jeal-ousy, and sometimes hatred and abuse. All the strength and value a common faith can bring are lost in such a situation.

What Values Are Lost in a Part-Member Marriage?

It is generally when the problems connected with children and their rearing arise that the lack of a single faith creates the greatest stress.

First, there is the problem of whether or not to have children. Without a firm belief in the plan of salvation, the presence of children in a family may not even seem de-sirable. They may be looked upon as a burden, a necessary evil. It is only when a man and woman desire children and love each other enough to commit their lives to each other for the purpose of bearing and rearing children that they experience a full measure of love in marriage. Wanting and having children are a large part of the tie that binds.

If the couple desires children, loves them, and wants the best in life for them, a difference in religion really becomes important. Then critical questions of an eternal nature concerning which church they should be reared in must be answered. Each parent may feel his church is right and best and may want the children reared in that faith which they now cherish so much. Possibly neither will give in, so the children grow up without training and are incapable of experiencing faith in God and his purposes for them in mortality. The *Harvard Study* indicated this was certainly so.

Children sense this difference in belief and the distress and upheaval it is causing in their home. It worries them and interferes with wholesome personality development. It may give them strong feelings of inferiority and a sense of insecurity toward all life. It may even cause them to hate one or both of their parents. Unhappy homes have a strong influence on the children in their own homes later on. Happy husbands and wives do not come from unhappy homes, as a rule. Therefore, dissension because of religion may be a great handicap in several ways.

In the course of life, most families must face disappointments of various kinds and degrees. Serious illness and death will likely cast their gloom over the family circle at some time. All faithful Latter-day Saints know how comforting it is to turn to the priesthood, the bishop, the stake president or even one of the General Authorities, in these hours of trial and seeming defeat.

But if the parents are inactive, or one or the other does not share a common belief in the powers of the priesthood, its advice, council, and blessings are denied in the hour of dire need. How much more comforting it is when parents can stand side by side in full faith as members of the priest-hood administer to a sick child. How reassuring it is to a child to have its daddy administer a blessing by virtue of the priesthood he holds and honors. Without a unity of faith these hours, days, and sometimes months and years of tribulation are filled with a feeling of defeat and bewilderment. With a unity of faith these trials are build-ers of love, loyalty, patience, and courage and may well prepare the way for a much greater reward in the eternities.

In part-member marriages children often drift even farther than their parents from those goals, beliefs, and standards which will lead to exaltation. The father or mother may be greatly distressed but can do nothing about it because of the opposition of the other parent. His feel-ings may be even more agonizing than those of a parent who watches his child drift helplessly out to sea in a boat which the child has entered and accidentally cast adrift because it did not understand the danger of its actions.

The late Elder John A. Widtsoe of the Council of the Twelve has summarized the whole problem rather well in the following words:

Above physical charm, love is begotten by quali-ties, often subtle, of mind and spirit. The beautiful face may hide an empty mind; the sweet voice may utter coarse words; the lovely form may be illmannered;

the women of radiant beauty and kindly form may be untolerable bores on nearer acquaintanceship, or the person who looks so attractive may really have no faults, may excel us in knowledge and courtesy; yet he is not our kind; his ways are not ours. Under either condition, love wilts in its first stage.

Falling in love is always from within, rather than from without. That is, physical attractiveness must be reinforced with mutual and spiritual harmony if true love is to be born and have long life. The man and his wife, to make life secure, must have the same outlook on the major issues of life; they must grow in the same direction. If one is an infidel and the other a believer in God, the resulting disagreement of spirit will tend to drive the two apart despite greater physical attractions. The association of husband and wife is so close and intimate that every difference becomes evident and important. (*Evidences and Reconciliations.* John A. Widtsoe, pp. 237-238.)

As people grow older and see life in a different perspective their values change. *That which seemed so desirable in youth becomes of little or no value.* The counterfeits of love and life which glittered so brightly early in life lose their luster and appeal. Physical, material goals and objects become slippery and cannot be held as death, the real determiner of true worth, relentlessly approaches.

It is then that a difference in faith becomes most critical. By then the member of the Church may see no foundation has been laid for a celestial exaltation. There are no ties that bind father, mother and children together in an eternal family kingdom. Possibly children do not even believe in God. Instead of being drawn together in a warm bond of love as the final departure of life approaches, each

family member stands apart, already separated emotionally
and spiritually as they will soon be physically. For no
people is this as tragic as for the Latter-day Saint, who has
a testimony of the gospel. He can sense the overwhelming
emptiness of a future life lacking celestial blessings.

Try to picture yourself in these final scenes in life
before you decide to enter a part-member marriage?

In order that you may have some idea how seriously
the Catholic Church views marriage of one of its members
with a non-Catholic person there follows a form of the
Ante-Nuptial Contract and Promises to be signed by both
parties to such a part-member marriage. As you read it
through try to decide whether you would sign such an
agreement. Has it ever occurred to you that even though
you would not sign such an agreement at your marriage
that in the years that follow you may actually fulfill its
demands?

Ante-Nuptial Contract and Promises

To be signed in duplicate at the presence of the
priest by the parties entering a mixed marriage, and
by two witnesses.

To Be Signed *by the Non*-Catholic Party

I, the undersigned, not a member of the Catholic
Church, wishing to contract marriage with the Catholic
party whose signature is hereinafter affixed to this
mutual agreement, being of sound mind and perfectly
free, and only after understanding fully the import
of my action, do hereby enter into this mutual agreement, understanding that the execution of this agreement and the promises therein contained are made
in contemplation of and in consideration for the con-

sent, marriage and consequent change of status of the hereinafter mentioned Catholic party, and I, therefore, hereby agree:

1. That I will not interfere in the least with the free exercise of the Catholic party's religion.

2. That I will adhere to the doctrine of the sacred indissolubility of the marriage bond, so that I cannot contract a second marriage while my consort is still alive, even though a civil divorce may have been obtained;

3. That all the children, both boys and girls, that may be born of this union shall be baptized and educated solely in the faith of the Roman Catholic Church, even in the event of the death of my Catholic consort. In case of dispute, I furthermore, hereby fully agree that the custody of all the children shall be given to such guardians as to assure the faithful execution of this covenant and promise;

4. That I will lead a married life in conformity with the Law of God and the teaching of the Catholic Church regarding birth control, realizing fully the attitude of the Catholic Church in this regard;

5. That no other marriage ceremony shall take place before or after this ceremony by the Catholic priest.

In testimony of which agreement, I do hereby solemnly swear that I will observe the above agreement and faithfully execute the promises wherein contained, and do now affix my signature in approval thereof.

Signature of the non-Catholic party

Address   City or Town

To Be Signed by the Catholic Party

I, the undersigned, a member of the Catholic Church, wishing to contract marriage with the non-Catholic party whose signature is affixed above to

this mutual agreement, being of sound mind and perfectly free, and only after understanding fully the import of my action, do hereby enter into this mutual
agreement, understanding that the execution of this
agreement and the promises therein contained are
made in contemplation of and in consideration for the
consent, marriage and consequent change of my status,
and I, therefore, hereby agree:

1. That I shall have all my children, both boys and
    girls, that may be born of this union, baptized and
    educated solely in the faith of the Roman Catholic
    Church. I understand that in case of my death,
    or in the event of a dispute, the custody of all the
    children shall be given to such guardians as to as-
    sure the faithful execution of this covenant and
    promise;
2. That I will practice my Catholic religion faithfully
    and will strive, especially by example, prayer and
    the frequentation of the Sacraments, to bring about
    the conversion of my consort;
3. That I will lead a married life in conformity with
    the Law of God and the teaching of the Catholic
    Church regarding birth control, realizing fully the
    attitude of the Catholic Church in this regard;
4. That no other marriage ceremony shall take place
    before or after this ceremony by the Catholic priest.

                    Signature of the Catholic party
                Address   City or Town
Signed in the presence of:
                            Witness
                            Witness

I, the undersigned, do hereby attest that the parties
whose signatures are affixed to the above agreement
and promises appeared before me personally on the

given date, and fully understanding the import, and meaning of the aforementioned agreement and promises, freely entered into this agreement and signed the above in my presence.

(Pastor—Assistant)

Date:

TWO COPIES of this form should be filled in and sent to the chancery. One copy, when duly signed, dated, and sealed by the Chancellor, will be returned to the priest to be kept in the parish archive: the other copy will be retained in the Chancery. See "Synodus Dioecesana Sancti Ludovici Septima — 1929" (Page 54 No. 95 under 2).

—***—

(From *Marriage for Moderns*, Second Edition by H. A. Bowman. Copyright, 1948. Courtesy of McGraw-Hill Book Co.)

To conclude this section on the problems connected with part-member marriage there follow two letters to Elder Mark E. Petersen of the Council of the Twelve. No comment on them is necessary. As you read them you will notice that their message is plain and very much to the point.

Dear Elder Petersen:

This Saturday was to have been my wedding day. It isn't now. Why? Because I attended conference last Sunday and I listened to you talk on temple marriage. The young man I had intended to marry, although he is a wonderful person, is not a Mormon. I thought perhaps I could change him after we are married. Now I can't even marry him and it is your fault. I don't really feel like saying thank you for your talk because in a way I resent it—but I don't really. I do want to say thank you because, although

I already knew what I should do, your talk made me change my mind. I can't marry outside of the church. I don't really want to, although I love Bob very much. I'm sure your words were inspired and I felt that they were the answer to my prayers. Thanks for saying what you did. Of course, if I am an "old maid" it will be your fault!

I would like to get a copy of your talk if one is available so that Bob can read it, and perhaps it will make a difference. I don't really know but it's worth a try. He believes so many things about the church, but the Word of Wisdom is holding him back because he believes it would take away his rights. Maybe someday he will change his mind. However, I'm sure that by reading your talk he would understand better how I feel.

Thank you again for keeping me from making a serious mistake. I know my mother and dad will be very happy to know that I am not getting married Saturday. Please send me a copy of your talk as soon as possible.

Sincerely,

Dear Elder Petersen:

As I listened to your address today, I wished so deep in my heart that I had listened to similar advice ten years ago. At the age of 22 I married a non-Mormon. I had dated good Mormon boys, but, although I had respect for them, they had failed to "sweep me off my feet." I knew the moment I met this fellow that he was the one for me. I know now that I could have been happier at the end of ten years had I married one of the other boys. I don't think I would have loved either of them as much as I do my husband, but love doesn't bring happiness of itself alone. One can be very much in love and still be unhappy.

The time has come when my duty is first to my children. We can no longer spend our Sundays at hunting or visiting. My children *need* to go to church. My husband is willing that I should take them, but I must go alone. We are separated in the one thing that could bring us the most joy (worshipping as a family).

I can see my marriage slowly slipping away from me. Our central interests are different. He likes dogs and sports, mine must be church and children. I must take the children slowly to me and away from him. We have no common ground on which to meet in time of trial and need. Couples who cannot pray together can seldom *talk* to each other. The loneliness I feel these days is almost more than I can bear. The worst part of the whole situation is the *conflicts* with yourself. Knowing that your *duty* is to the children and the church and, yet, *wanting* the companionship of your husband. I sincerely hope you will continue to impress these important facts on our youth. I don't believe this subject can be stressed too much to our young boys and girls. May God be with me that I may find a solution to my problem. I sincerely hope He can help me do the best with the mistake I have made.

Sincerely,

CHAPTER NINE

WHY IS CHARACTER IMPORTANT TO A SUCCESSFUL MARRIAGE?

Hermits do not need to worry about character. It is only when people live, associate, and work with other people that they need character. *Character has been defined as the ability to live according to the rules and habits of the society in which you find yourself.* Unless one has this ability, he or she cannot live in a complex society like our culture and be happy and make a worthwhile contribution.

While a family has only a few members and is not too complex, it is highly intimate. The family members live so closely together and share so much of their personal lives that it takes excellent character or self-control to live happily and successfully in this human relationship.

As Latter-day Saints we are tied together even more closely in eternal marriage. This covenant places upon us the need to live even more fully all the principles of the gospel. Unless a person has good character, he or she will not be able to abide by the covenants faithful Latter-day Saints make.

Character, sufficient for a successful eternal marriage, is a developed capacity. It is developed by living, from childhood, two great laws, on which all growth and happiness depend.

Jesus himself said they were the basis of exaltation. These are the two laws of which he spoke:

"Thou shalt love the Lord thy God with all thy might, mind and strength. This is the first and great commandment; the second is like unto it; thou shalt love thy neighbour as thyself."

People who have kept these laws have lived a certain way, even from childhood. They have learned to have consideration for the feelings, goals, and efforts of others. They have been taught and have accepted the idea they have a mission on this earth and that this is the only real reason for mortal existence. They have been helpful family members, assuming their share of work and responsibility. They have participated in Church auxiliaries and kept the law of tithing and the Word of Wisdom to the best of their ability. They have taken advantage of their school opportunities and been contributing citizens in their school student bodies. The girls have done all they can to prepare themselves to be true helpmates to their husbands, and inspiring, loving mothers for the eternal spirits who will some day come to their homes as babies. The boys have been active and worthy bearers of the priesthood as they were ordained deacons, teachers, and priests. They have been clean of speech, honest in their dealings with others, and reverent toward things sacred and holy. They have always considered themselves as full partners with God the Father and shunned all things which made them unworthy to be such.

People of good character are kind, sympathetic, and helpful. They have learned to substitute cooperative understanding and friendly attitudes for brutality and aggressiveness so common in the world. They are definitely interested in the welfare of others and are constantly seeking ways to help them.

Without this developed capacity to live with others, marriage is likely to be difficult and often unsuccessful. Young people should strive to acquire good character so they in turn can expect it from those whom they will marry. When young people who have not developed their character want to marry, serious problems arise. Sometimes they think they can quickly erase their character deficiencies because they want to and have promised to change.

Can People Change by Just Wanting To?

John had been a "character" all his life. He did nothing but cause trouble in school, and as a result his grades were low. Profanity was the rule and not the exception in his speech. He rarely went to church or performed his duties in the priesthood. He always had to have a drink or two before he went to a dance, and on occasions he became disgustingly drunk. Money burned holes in his pockets, and he spent it quickly for the first thing which caught his fancy. He had no respect for his father and mother and spoke of them as the "old man" and the "old woman." The girls whom he dated felt heavy petting was not too great a price to pay for his favors and attentions and he was as likely as not to speak about girls with little respect.

Then at twenty-three he met Sue. He was fascinated by her sweet, demure ways. They were so different from the brassy manners of his previous girl friends of whom he was now tired. He begin to feel wonderful when he was around her, and he continued to feel that way after the few dates she would give him. He no longer felt a desire to talk about her in the manner in which he had talked about his former girl friends. But there were several things which disturbed him. She wouldn't take a drink, not even a sociable one. She objected in various ways to his smoking. In no uncertain terms she told him that vulgarity and profanity were absolutely out when he was with her. She had even mentioned going to church. A time or two she had tried to talk with him about his activities in the Church.

This relationship went on for some time. Gradually John fell desperately in love with this lovely creature who radiated something which to him was so delightful, so desirable, so clean, and so uplifting that he felt life would not be worthwhile if he could not win her as his bride.

One memorable evening, after a Gold and Green ball, at which they had both enjoyed themselves greatly, he asked her to share her life with him. Sue was stunned. She had not known that he felt so serious about her. John was only a teacher; he had no interest in the Church. In addition he still smoked and drank. She could see they could not have a temple marriage.

After a few moments of reflective thought, Sue outlined these conditions and the fact that she would never marry out of the temple. Then John really became ardent. He vowed that if Sue would only marry him he would certainly change. Sue would be a strength to him and keep him on the path of clean living. Then sometime, soon, they would be married in the temple. With a pleading look in his eyes that threatened to melt all resistance in Sue's womanly heart, he waited for an answer.

What would have been your answer? The offer was made in good faith, but do you believe it would have been a basis for marriage in the light of Sue's goals? When promises are made in order to get something, can we rely on them? Does a marriage built on promises of this type contain the seeds of disappointment and failure? Would Sue have this boy's soul on her hands if she turned him down?

How Easy Is It to Change One's Character?

It is probable that the plea, "I'll change if you will marry me," is quite common among those who have lived lives of disobedience and heedless selfishness. The question now arises, under what conditions can character deficiencies be made up? Can the desired but undeveloped capacities be quickly acquired by wishing for them? That people can change traits of personality and character no one will deny. The question is, does the desire to do so, expressed in a highly emotional state, suffice? For the Latter-day Saints there is even more to be considered. For them to live with their fellow members requires control in matters which the world does not think important. They need a much more highly developed capacity to live, not only with earthly inhabitants but also in active partnership with their Heavenly Father, even in mortal life.

How Are Habits Formed and How Are They Changed?

It is a known fact that the longer an individual responds to a stimulus in a certain way the more difficult it is to make any other response. When this response has become tied in with strong satisfactions in other areas of living, it becomes a web of unbelievable strength and complexity. Only professionals such as psychiatrists, psychologists, social workers, etc., know how long it takes to rebuild a personality with new habits and traits. In many instances the time, money, effort, and difficulties involved seem to make it impractical. In some manner the same amount of effort and energy it took to create a habit must be expended to break it. If you have traveled down the wrong fork of the road for ten miles, you have to go back ten miles to get on the right road. True repentance is not quick and easy. Those who think it is have not kept track of individuals who have resolved to change and have failed.

Character is relatively stable. This very fact protects those who have consistently applied restraint to their desires and have practised habits of good character. They have an increased power of resistance and a lessening of the power of temptation in their lives. Unfortunately wrong living has just the opposite effect. It gives temptation more power and attraction and intensifies the struggle to do right. Bad habits have a definite tendency and capacity to persist. They can be changed only by the necessary determination and persistence.

The sensible boy or girl will realize that people sometimes say they will change merely to get something they greatly desire. You have probably done so in your lifetime. When people do this, they are no doubt wholly sincere because the goal they seek makes the change seem most desirable. However, when they get what they want, the need for the change ceases to exist, and they go back to their old habits and attitudes.

One young woman was heart-broken when her husband failed to keep the promises he had made before their marriage—a promise to be willing to have a large family; a promise never to interfere with her practice of her religion; a promise to study the Book of Mormon. Whenever she reminded him, "But you promised!" he laughed and said, "That was before marriage."

Is There a Way to Know Whether or Not a Person Will Change?

There are some questions you might ask yourself if you are ever called upon to make a decision in this matter. These could be:

1. How long has the boy had his bad habit? The older it is, the more difficult it will be to eliminate.

2. What is his attitude toward it? Is he really ashamed of it or does he regard it highly? The desire to be rid of a bad habit is half the battle.

3. Does he come from a home where this and other bad habits and attitudes have been practised and defended? If so, they may be deeply ingrained in his thinking and feeling.

4. How active has he been in the Church in early youth? A good foundation makes a change in direction more likely.

5. Has the individual tried to change in other fields of living? Was he successful more often than not? The answer to this question would indicate whether will power and self-determination are present.

6. What kind of friends does the boy have? How long has he had this kind of friends? Friends have a strong influence, and it is hard to leave them and their influence and way of life behind.

7. Has the boy a desire for fine, clean things in other aspects of life, or is his taste cheap and vulgar all the way through? Desires and habits reinforce each other and assist or hinder the acquiring of new ones in other areas.

Should One Spouse Try to Make the Other Over?

The strengthening assistance and moral support of a loved one in overcoming a bad habit cannot be denied. However, the self-respect of a husband or wife is destroyed when one's mate is constantly trying to make him over. Each individual must take the initiative in determining the pattern of his or her life. Only in this way can each maintain respect for each other. Respect is the foundation of enduring love. Without respect, love dies.

In summary it can be said that without character one cannot live happily and successfully with others. Only you can create your character. It is one of life's most precious achievements. As with all things of value it grows slowly and is not easy to come by. It needs constant cultivation. Wishing for it will not produce it.

"I'm ready!"

CHAPTER TEN

WHAT IS THE BEST AGE FOR MARRIAGE?

You have no doubt noticed that this question is often good for a stimulating discussion which at times creates more heat than light. This is because there are so many angles and points of view from which to consider the problem. Most of them are based on how people *feel* about the matter. Teenagers, parents, judges, psychologists, Church leaders, and others each have a different interest to defend.

In order to bring your point of view into a more definite focus there follows a series of statements on the proper age for marriage. Which of the following do you accept? One should marry only under the following conditions:

1. As soon as you feel you have fallen in love.

2. As young as possible so you can grow up with your children.

3. The boy should be at least 25.

4. A boy should get his army training, a mission, and schooling behind him before he thinks of marriage.

5. Girls should wait until they are at least twenty.

6. As soon as you can earn enough to live on.

7. Every girl should have enough training to be able to support herself in case she has to support herself and her children.

8. People mature at different ages so you should get married whenever you feel mature.

What Is the Trend in the Age for Marriage?

A discussion of the foregoing problems will probably reveal the fact that on the basis of opinion alone no agreement can be achieved. Therefore it might be helpful to study trends in marriage age and the success in marriage of these different age groups.

Statistical studies from census reports and other investigations reveal a definite trend toward younger marriages in our country. With plentiful jobs, relatively good wages for unskilled labor, early dating, and the widespread custom of going steady, teenagers seem more inclined to plan for marriage before they are twenty.

The next question is whether this is a desirable or undesirable trend. If it is bad, it will show deficiencies no matter where it is tried. In this regard it is interesting to note what has happened in Japan, a land of customs and culture very foreign to ours.

The Tokyo *Japan Digest* reports that "the Domestic Affairs court statistics reveal that marriage for love, which became fashionable after World War II, is far less durable than the traditional marriage arranged by a go-between." (Oscar F. Gavilovich. Compiled from newspapers around the world. Quoted from *Deseret News,* Oct. 1958.)

The paper attributes the failure of love marriages to the fact that "nowadays young Japanese marry as soon as they fall in love; before they have time to consider family traditions and ties."

This is what Samuel Grafton had to say in *McCall's Magazine*.

The lads and maidens who thus marry in their teens adopt an extremely risky design for living; their divorce rate is appalling. (A bride under twenty has three times the chances of being divorced as a girl who marries between the ages of 22 and 24.) Even when a teenage marriage does work out—as in some cases, touchingly and movingly, it does—it must sometimes go through a strange testing period social workers uniformly describe as sad. After their marriage has caused the initial splash of glamorous excitement, the typical teenage couple, say a boy 17 and a girl 16, often find they quickly lose their teenage friends, who have other interest: games, going out for sports, dating. But the young married pair cannot make adult friends. They have as the sociologists say, no "peer group" to which they belong and in which they can move as equals. If nearby are other teenage married couples with whom they are compatible, friendship may continue; but kids of different background who were not buddies at school do not become friends on the basis of the fact that marriage has set in. Sociologists tend to agree that, particularly in the younger age groups, 16 and 17, teenage married couples are among the loneliest people in America; they are in a kind of limbo for one or two years, their marriages undergoing a unique strain, *to which marriages at a later age are not subject.* There is no social group with which a boy of 17, married to a girl of 16 who is having a baby, can make contact. Frequently such married youngsters are thrust back on their own parents as the only friends. Often, after a year or so of teenage marriage, an intense desire flares up in one partner or the other to be a teenager again and have the parties and fun once more. (*McCall's Magazine.* Samuel Grafton. Nov. 1959, pp. 118-119.)

Life Magazine recently carried an article on this trend toward child marriages resulting from the present dating tendencies of American youth. After showing what leads

up to these tragic marriages, the article discussed the divorces which result. Judge Willard Galting of Charlotte,
North Carolina, was quoted as saying:

"Teenage marriage has almost no possibility of succeeding. Ninety percent are total failures." (*Deseret
News*, Mark E. Petersen, Oct. 17, 1959.)

There seems to be little doubt that age plays a vital
role in the failure or success of marriage. How important
it is for you to understand this fact! When you realize the
risk involved in early marriage you will be willing to wait
until you are at least twenty before you take this all-important step, if you are wise.

Why Is Maturity Important In Marriage?

Maturity is just another word for being able and prepared to assume responsibility in life.

It will be well to substitute the word *maturity* for the
concept of age, at least in some aspects of this problem.
Age and maturity usually are very closely related. To
think differently could cause one to reach some false conclusions.

When we speak of maturity for marriage in this
study we will have to speak of it against the background
of the culture in which we live.

People who live close to the animal level, in a simple
society where food and shelter are available to all on a
take-and-use basis, need little more than physical maturity.
In such societies there is little need for personality development, education, culture, or social life. As civilizations
become more complex, the marriage age seems to rise. This
is because more development and maturity are necessary

to be a contented member of such a society. Our civilization has become quite complex. There is much stress on personal growth and development. It is not difficult to see how teens find that they are not equipped to live in such a culture as married people.

Age for marriage then is determined by the maturity necessary to live in the society or part of society in which one finds oneself. Our LDS society is in some respects more complex than that of the world in which we live. Members of the Church must then consider maturity from the standpoint of the goals they have in mind as they seek celestial exaltation. The aims of the world are not a suitable measuring unit. The best age for you to marry is when you have reached the physical, economic, emotional, and spiritual maturity which will enable you to eventually accomplish the purpose for which you were sent to earth.

When Are People Physically Mature Enough to Be Married?

Physical maturity is determined only in part by height and weight. Not all organs and structures of the human body reach their full development at the same time. You are acquainted with the clumsiness and seeming lack of co-ordination which many young people experience. They may be heavier and taller than their parents, but they lack the co-ordination, endurance, and physical self-control of an older person. This is due to the fact that there is an unbalance in the development of the bones and muscles. It is amazing how a few years of maturing give young people physical poise, confidence, and strength.

Girls who marry too young tend to age more rapidly. The organs of their bodies, the tendons, ligaments, and muscles which are involved in child-bearing are not mature. They function but tend to weaken and to break down and are unable to give the most effective service over the lifetime of the very young mother.

Those who have made thorough studies of physical maturity believe that girls, generally speaking, are not mature until they are about twenty years of age. Men reach their physical prime at about twenty-six but may be relatively mature around twenty-two. From the standpoint of physical maturity then, these seem to be good ages for marriage.

When Are People Emotionally Mature Enough to Marry?

Emotionally mature people possess the following characteristics: (1) he or she can stand pain and suffering with courage and faith; (2) he or she can pursue goals in life which require patience and persistence; (3) he or she takes a deep interest in others and is concerned about their welfare and happiness.

People mature emotionally when they change from "me" to "we" people. It is plainly evident that some people never grow up emotionally. A close study of the lives of unhappy, unsuccessful persons would very likely reveal emotional immaturity as the core of their problems.

Young people in their teens are generally "me" minded. They have not had enough opportunity for self-control and unselfish service to achieve emotional maturity. They are generally more concerned about themselves than about others, even their parents. Teens are energetic and like to go from one activity to another. They like to do things on the spur of the moment. To them, people who say "wait a minute, let's look this thing over carefully," are "old fogies" or "wet blankets." It is difficult for them to wait for rewards. One man has said they are "Esau" people. From your study of the Old Testament you will know what this means. Esau was willing to sell his birth-right for physical satisfaction!

Until this age has passed and young people have danced, played, and had a satisfactory social life, they find it hard to settle down to the routine and sacrifices of marriage. When one's age group is still deep in the whirl of school dances, plays, operettas, ball games, and club activities, it is most difficult to pass it all by and spend one's evenings at home with a colicky baby. This social pull is so strong that it is a great threat to youthful marriages. It seems dangerous to move too far ahead of one's age group emotionally and socially.

What Economic Problems Should the Young Couple Be Able to Solve?

How often have you heard it said that two can live as cheaply as one? Do you believe it? Many have entered marriage believing it. Evidently there is something wrong with this conclusion because discord over money matters is high on the list of problems which lead to divorce. The fact that certain young people will accept such a statement might be a good indication of their immaturity in the area of economics.

What then are some of the preparations young people should make in order that money matters will not destroy their marriage?

1. Enough education, training, experience, and maturity to earn a living and to be able to increase those earnings when the financial requirements of the family increase. In this regard young people often make a great error in judgment. A high school boy doesn't need much training or education to work in a grocery store, a service station, or a car-washing establishment. The wages he earns may be adequate at his age. In fact he may feel and appear to be quite rich compared to those who are still in school, struggling along on what they have earned during the summer, or what they may receive from their parents. The former boy may have a pretty good car and enough money to show his dates a good time. The girls may be greatly impressed by his financial power. This may be so true that one of them can be talked into marriage.

But after marriage this picture often changes radically. This change may come slowly or suddenly depending on circumstances. It is generally a rude awakening to a young couple to find out that rent, food, clothing, medicine, and other necessities of life (which they expected from their parents as a matter of course) make the earnings from unskilled work inadequate. Under these circumstances, Worry parks himself in the little love nest and squawks away, night and day, in irritating, discordant notes. Soon the young people start snapping at each other, never realizing that it is their financial condition and not their personalities which is causing the discord. How can immature love withstand this unwelcome 'worry bird'?

Even if they live successfully through the early years of economic difficulty, they will find the pressure increasing as children come, and the amount necessary for the

"I wish we had waited!"

basic needs of life increases. Young men should be as well trained and prepared as possible to earn a living for those who will later depend on them.

2. A young couple should have about the same economic background. One's spending habits are deeply ingrained. People who have grown up with all the money they want will find it difficult to count pennies—if they must. Boys of modest means and earning possibilities who marry girls from wealthy homes may face an unusual problem. Very often the wife urges the young husband to accept the well-meant offers of financial help from her family. If the boy accepts, he may feel it is a reflection on his role as breadwinner and indicates he is failing as a man. If he refuses to accept the help, it may be impossible to maintain the standard of living to which his wife feels entitled. In either instance there are feelings of guilt and resentment which make marriage difficult and unsatisfying.

People from greatly different levels of economy frequently have tastes and standards which tend to keep the young couple apart. The size, styles, and decorations of the wealthy homes may seem a necessity to the girl who comes from such a home. She may feel deprived and socially insecure if she cannot have such a home in which to live and entertain friends. She may be accustomed to certain types of entertainment and travel. Anything less may prove uninteresting and inadequate. On the other hand a girl who comes from a more modest home may not have the skill to decorate and maintain the highly styled homes of the wealthy. She may also meet resentment when her marriage opens the doors to certain social circles which are reserved for those who are not considered outsiders. Such a girl may actually find it a burden to enjoy the social activities of such groups.

These differences in taste and living standards are not necessarily a reflection on anyone's character and personal worth. Lovely, faithful people are found on all economic levels. But considerable differences in financial background can cause a great strain on marriage.

3. Young people should be spiritually and emotionally mature enough to accept a standard of living which may be lower than that of their parental homes.

The era of easy credit which exists presently in the United States is a menace to all who do not know how to use it wisely and sparingly. Credit is a crutch too often used by those whose incomes are low. Credit, plus an inadequate income, plus a standard of living like that of the parents (who have had twenty-five to thirty-five years to achieve their present financial position in life) equals disaster. Such disaster would be avoided if young married people would adopt a standard of living based on the following philosophy expressed by Elder Spencer W. Kimball on this important topic:

> Happiness is a strange commodity. It cannot be purchased with money, and yet it is bought with a price. It is not dependent upon houses, or lands, or flocks, or degrees, or position, or comforts, for many of the most unhappy people in all the world have these. The millionaire has comforts and luxuries, but he has no happiness unless he has paid the same price for it that you can also pay. Often the richest are the most unhappy; if you think that ease and comfort and money are necessary for your happiness, ask your parents and others whose lives are in the autumn. They will

generally tell you that the happiest days were not the ones when they were retired, with a palatial home, two cars in the garage, and money with which to travel around the world, but their joyous days were those when they, too planned and schemed for the where-withal to make ends meet; when they had their little ones about them and were wholly absorbed in family life and church work.

And so, Mary and John, you may live in a single room or a small cabin and be happy. You may ride the bus or walk instead of riding in luxurious cars, and still be happy. You may wear your clothes more than a single season and still be happy.

The treasure house of happiness is unlocked and remains open to those who use the following two keys: the first, you must live the gospel of Jesus Christ unit-edly in its purity and simplicity—not a halfhearted compliance but a hewing to the line. And this means an all-out devoted consecration to the great program of salvation and exaltation in an orthodox manner. The second, you must forget yourself and love your companion more than yourself. If you do these things, happiness will be yours in great and never-failing abundance. (*Improvement Era*, Spencer W. Kimball, February 1949.)

Economic maturity means a person has the ability to live within his means; to be satisfied with a modest home, if necessary.

When Are People Spiritually Mature Enough for Marriage?

Would you say you are a spiritual person? Have you ever tried to define spirituality? People talk about it a great deal, but when asked exactly what it means, they have a difficult time putting it in words.

In order that you may see this phase of maturity in its relationship to marriage consider the following: *Spirituality is the desire and ability to live in harmony with the laws and purposes of God.* Such a person hungers for friendship and close association with our Heavenly Father and delights in assisting in the building of his kingdom. Such a person holds sacred the power to be a parent. Such a person strives to keep all his urges and drives in check being careful not to use them for pure excitement or entertainment. A person who is spiritually mature reserves the physical expressions of the procreative urge for his chosen mate with whom he intends to accept, in full love and affection, the responsibilities of marriage.

Whenever there is a choice between God's way and the world's, the spiritually mature choose God's way. Adam Noah, Abraham, Isaac, Jacob, Joseph, and many others in the Old Testament are good examples. Jesus is, of course the supreme example. In our day there have been many people who have shown spiritual maturity. The Prophet Joseph Smith stands at the head. Behind him stands a great concourse of Saints. Are some of them your ancestors. Do not the stories of their faithful dedication to God's work inspire you?

Measure your own spiritual maturity by the following examples:

1. A very popular high school girl who had been elected cheerleader was married in the temple during her senior year. During basketball season the question arose in her mind about wearing her garments while acting as a cheerleader. Should she wear her abbreviated costume without the garments? Should she make a new cheer-

leader uniform which would not be so revealing? Or should she give up her position as cheerleader? This particular girl felt so strongly about her endowment in the temple that she gave up being cheerleader. Some will say she was foolish. What would you have done?

2. You are taking a test. Everyone, well almost everyone it seems, is cheating. You may fail unless you also cheat. What will you do? Cheat and get a grade? Or be honest, possibly failing, and be able to say you are an honest person when you go to get a temple recommend?

3. You are a boy in his sophomore year in college. You are about ready to start your study of medicine after a struggle to gain admittance to a very desirable professional school. The bishop wants to call you on a mission. What is your answer?

4. You are a girl. A boy with a fine car and almost an unlimited allowance from his father wants you to be his steady. He smokes once in a while, swears to be cute, and makes light of his priesthood duties. He goes to Church sometimes but gets little out of it. Many girls consider him a real "catch."

Another boy wants to date you. He is saving his money for a mission. Once in a while he gets the family car. He can't take his girl friends on any expensive dates. He is nice looking but definitely not flashy. He is a bit shy and doesn't have the "line" the first boy has. Which would you choose? Why?

5. You suddenly realize you are not going to have enough money to last you through the school year if you pay your tithing. Would you pay your tithing?

These are samples of problems you will face. Your answer will indicate the degree of your spiritual maturity. These problems are not as difficult as some you will face after marriage. They will require immeasurably more faith and courage. Spiritual maturity is most vital if you are not to be overwhelmed by the adjustments you have to make in marriage. Spiritual maturity does not come with the marriage ceremony, even when performed in the temple. It is an outstanding achievement, something of which you can be proud. It does not come in its fulness until the end of a faithful life, but a definite measure of it must be had at the time of marriage if the marriage is to be truly successful.

Is It Possible to Give the Exact Age When One Should Marry?

You can see that it is difficult to set a definite age when all marriages are most likely to succeed. Physical, social, economic, and spiritual maturity are needed. *However, it should again be stressed that age and maturity are probably fairly well correlated.*

Drs. Skidmore and Cannon, in their book, *Building Your Marriage,* have made a summary of five research studies as to the best age for marriage. The following conclusions speak for themselves:

(1) Rounded maturity usually takes time. Emotional, social, economic, and vocational, and spiritual maturity usually develops over a number of years. Personality patterns and philosophy of life stabilize as one passes from adolescence into adult life. (2) Until personality patterns stabilize and until various forms of maturity are achieved, the person does not know himself and is unable to judge effectively the values

he desires in a mate. (3) Partners in youthful marriages are more likely to grow away from each other
than couples who marry in their twenties. (4) Infatu-
ation and physical factors are more likely to lead to
marriage among teen-agers than among other age
groups. Older persons pay more attention to the total
personality and background. (5) Rational study of
marriage and mate selection occurs more frequently
among those who marry at later ages than among those
who marry earlier. (6) Premature marriages may be
a symptom of unhappiness and may constitute an
attempt to escape from reality rather than to face and
solve problems. (7) Many early marriages are hastily
contracted on short acquaintance. (8) Early marriages
are more likely to have the opposition of parents and
relatives. (9) The teen-age wife is likely to be unpre-
pared for the duties of managing a household, and the
teen-age husband unable to earn enough to support
a family. (*Building Your Marriage*. Anthon S. Cannon and Rex A. Skidmore. 1951. Harper & Brothers,
New York, N. Y., pp. 246-248.)

CHAPTER ELEVEN

WHAT ROLE DOES PERSONALITY PLAY IN MARRIAGE?

The ambition of most Americans is to have a "winning" personality. Books on how to obtain it have a wide sale. The feeling is that a "good" personality will assure social and business success. But the understanding many people have of personality is often too closely related to its presentation in advertisements in magazines and newspapers. These picture girls with "poor" personalities who suddenly lose this handicap by using a certain mouthwash, toothpaste, or hair shampoo. It is just that simple — or so these advertisements say.

But psychologists know this is far from the truth. They define personality as the sum total of one's adjustment to one's environment from the day of birth. This would include one's characteristic attitudes toward others, his habits of thought and ways of expression, his interests, and ambitions, his plan for life, and his attitude toward life in general. For an example of two kinds of personality and the difficulties involved, let us look in on a young couple as they sit at supper:

"Let's go to the Mutual dance with the Joneses tonight," wheedled Mary.

"Oh, Mary, how often have I told you that I want to stay home after I get through the day's work?" rejoined John a bit impatiently.

"But, John, you are alone all day at the laboratory. I

should think you would want to get out and mingle with people."

"People bore me," complained her husband. "I would rather stay home and read a book and that's what I am going to do!"

John turned his back to Mary and settled down to reading his book.

Mary was hurt and upset. She dabbed at the tears which came into her eyes as she walked into her kitchen to think things over. It all seemed so confusing. John had not been this way before their marriage. True, he had often spoken of how he loved to walk alone in the woods, or by the lake shore, or sit alone before a fireplace. It had taken considerable urging to get him to go to certain social functions. He did not enjoy himself too much as a rule, unless he could get in a corner and strike up a conversation with some person on a scientific topic. But he had danced and seemed to enter into social activities with considerable enthusiasm at times.

Had Mary been a trained psychologist, she would have quickly known that John was a person who leaned toward introversion. Had she examined her own personality closely, she would have sensed that she was inclined to extroversion.

Before marriage these inclinations may not seem to be highly important; after marriage they play an important role.

What Are the Important Personality Types and How Do They Affect Marriage?

As people grow up, they tend to develop what is known

as "central tendency." That is, they tend to respond fairly consistently to the different experiences in their environment. In the preceding example we have two main types of personal adjustment to life. John represents the introvert; Mary, the extrovert. Not all people have such well-defined tendencies. Most of us are ambiverts; that is, we may be introverted in some respects and extroverted in others. We can adjust comfortably either way if the need arises. But if there is a strong persistent tendency one way or the other, this tendency calls for careful consideration.

What Is the Basic Nature of the Introvert?

The introvert finds the center of his life within himself. He considers everything in the light of its affect on *his* life. He likes to stand on the side lines and watch. He resists being drawn into activity with others. He is likely to be shy and have only a small circle of intimate friends. Social events and parties are not in his line. He loves certain types of employment such as a laboratory technician, or a forest lookout, or any occupation where he works alone or with materials rather than with people. An introvert has a sharp conscience. He spends a great deal of time examining his motives and actions. Verily, the world turns around him and his own welfare.

How Does the Extrovert React to Life?

The extrovert is just the opposite of the introvert. Crowds thrill him and give him a "lift." He is the hail fellow well met. He is eternally busy trying to make people happy and comfortable wherever he finds them. He does not necessarily do this from unselfish motives. He may do it for selfish purposes and to inflate his own ego. But it is his approach to getting what he wants. He adjusts to changing groups very well. He must have a strong and steady diet of social activities. Clubs, organizations, church, and community activities interest him greatly. He is the teacher, the salesman, the politician, the individual who works with and for people. The extrovert is not inclined to worry about his mistakes and misfortunes. Tomorrow, he tells himself, will be a better day, and everything will turn out well. Life is to him a grand experience, especially if it includes lots of people and social activities.

What Happens When People of Widely Different Personality Types Marry?

During the limited contacts of courtship the differences in personality are not so important. If necessary, one can force an adjustment for an occasion or so. But after marriage the "central tendency" tends to shape the *whole* of the lives of the couple. Instead of complementing one another, widely different personality types tend to limit growth and enjoyment in married life. As people grow older, "central tendencies" become stronger and wield more influence.

There is another aspect of personality which should definitely be mentioned. It concerns the matter of what might be called "energy output." Sometimes people are mismated in this respect. The husband or wife may work, play, and live life generally at a much faster, harder, and more vigorous pace than the other mate. If the difference is too great, this condition can be very distressing. It is like trying to get two poorly matched horses to pull as a team.

If you have ever been around men who enter teams in the horse-pulling contests, so popular at fairs, you will have noted the great importance they attach to "matching." A marriage team also needs sensible matching in the main personality aspects of the two individuals involved.

How Can Courtship Assure a Matching of Personalities?

While courtship will be discussed at greater length a little later, it might be well to point out that one of its main functions is to determine the degree to which two young people may hope that their personalities will complement each other in marriage. If, as the courtship progresses, there is evidence that interests and enjoyment in life tend to go in opposite directions too often and too long, serious caution should be observed in entering such a marriage. When enjoyment of recreational interests, participation in church work, community service, and cultural activities vary widely and basically they may be love-destroying factors in marriage. Activities should bring couples closer together and not be a source of mutual irritation. If people have radically different viewpoints of life, like the introvert and extrovert, adjustment will be much more difficult and for some virtually impossible.

In conclusion, it should be stated that personality is not a matter of physical glamor, "cute" mannerisms, and a "smooth" line. One writer has described these as "a package whose wrappings are glamorous but which has no contents of value." During courtship the wrappings are most important, but it is the contents of the mind and soul of one's mate which must sustain love long after the wrappings have been discarded.

Young people should consider the personality of the mate they desire. Is it good from the standpoint of its ability to bring happy, abundant living into the family circle? Or is it superficial—just a delightful prelude to short-lived excitement? Take warning from the words of the cynic, Wilson Mizner: "The days just prior to marriage," he warned, "are like a snappy introduction to a tedious book."

Look Beyond the Surface

CHAPTER TWELVE

WHAT IS THE ROLE OF HEREDITY IN CREATING A HAPPY HOME AND FAMILY?

When people think of miracles, they generally think of events such as the children of Israel passing through the Red Sea dry-shod, healing of the sick, or raising the dead. These are regarded as miracles because they are beyond present human understanding. In order for an event to be classed as a miracle some people feel it must be sensational or of rare occurrence. But among people who have studied it, the process of the preparation of an earthly tabernacle, a body for the eternal inheritance and use of a spirit, is as great a miracle as is recorded. Yet it is an event which takes place many millions of times each year. How our Heavenly Father has provided the mechanism whereby the reproductive cell carries the characteristics of one's ancestors and makes their persistence p o s s i b l e through countless generations is something which remains a mystery to the minds of men. It is truly a miracle. When one looks upon the perfect body of a newborn babe—a body which has within it processes which no man or group of men can comprehend or duplicate—and when one realizes all has developed in a few months from two tiny cells so small that they cannot be seen with the naked eye, one can but marvel in silent awe at the intelligence of God, our Heavenly Father. This miracle of life should make us aware that our roles as co-creaters with God are the greatest power man possesses.

The purpose of this chapter is to examine the laws of this process only as far as such knowledge will help us use them intelligently, so that our parenthood will provide the most perfect bodies possible for the spirits which come to dwell with us.

The quality of one's heredity is determined by the genes from the father and the mother and the way they combine in the union of the reproductive cells. This proceeds on the basis of the order revealed in Mendel's law. This law states that "like begets like" when the characteristics are dominant enough in one or both parents. Some of these traits are dominant and appear with great certainty and regularity. Others are called recessive (from receding or going backward) and become operative only in cases where they are reinforced by recessive combinations from both parents. The terms *dominant* and *recessive* are important for our study. Some diseases, like Huntington's chorea (quite rare), are almost invariably inherited. They are wholly dominant. Others are almost never passed on from parent to child. They are recessive. Some are inherited only by the male children through the mothers. These are called sex-linked traits. The inheritability of most diseases lies somewhere between these extremes.

Some deficiencies, such as diabetes, can be made recessive if a person whose family heredity shows a more than normal frequency of this condition marries into a family in which it is virtually unknown. This is the most practical approach which can be made to the problem of avoiding burdening one's children with serious mental and physical weaknesses and deficiencies. As with everything else on this earth, there are imperfections at best in the

process of tabernacling spirits. Some of these occur without apparent reason. Such an incident is recorded by John.

> And as Jesus passed by, he saw a man which
> was blind from his birth.
>
> And his disciples asked him, saying, Master, who
> did sin, this man, or his parents, that he was born
> blind?
>
> Jesus answered, Neither hath this man sinned,
> nor his parents: but that the works of God should be
> made manifest in him.''
>
> (John 9:1-3.)

In these instances, love and patience with the handicapped one may be the only adjustment possible. The only
workable solution is to believe that the works of God will
sometime, somewhere, be made manifest if we show the
proper attitude toward the unfortunate one.

If there are serious, unfavorable physical or mental
conditions in a family which are constantly recurring, it
is most important to present the problem to a qualified
doctor or adequately trained eugenist. Not just anyone
will do; it should be a person who is fully and currently
informed. Friends, relatives, and unqualified people should
never be allowed to decide how important hereditary factors are in one's life. Experts can pretty well indicate the
mathematical chance of a condition being inherited under
certain conditions. The prospective parents can then decide whether or not they want to take this chance.

As you reach courting age, you should become aware
of the strength and weaknesses of your own heredity.
When courting starts, there should never be a commitment
to each other unless there has been time to determine dis-

creetly and quietly whether it would be well to combine the two heredities involved.

Two very fine Latter-day Saints have set a forthright pattern for young people in choosing their companions. In the August 1946 *Improvement Era*, is told the story of the marriage of David A. and Mina Murdock Broadbent.

When Oliver Wendell Holmes stated that if one wished to improve the race, one must begin with the grandmother, he did not realize the suggestion would be independently worked out by David A. and Mina Murdock Broadbent. Before they were married in the Manti Temple, May 1, 1901, each had made a careful study of the other's family and had felt it would be good to combine their heritage.

Twelve fine children were born to this couple. The children have filled twelve missions, thirty-four years in all. Every child has graduated from college, and all twelve children have been married in the temple.

Biblical history indicates the need for care in the selection of one's partner in marriage. Your own lineage had some notable people in it at the beginning. It is interesting to note the great care with which the mothers of this people, which was to be peculiar to the Lord, were chosen. First there was Sarah, wife of Abraham. She was so outstanding that the Pharaoh of Egypt wanted to marry her. She was the mother of Isaac. Through the inspiration of the Lord, Rebekah was obtained as a wife for Isaac. She became the mother of Jacob, prince of Israel. Jacob returned to his own land and won his beloved Rachel to whom was born Joseph. Joseph in turn became the father of Ephraim, from whom you are descended. These people knew they were a chosen people and were careful not to intermarry with the pagans among whom they lived. Of course the Lord knows the importance of the laws of heredity and so always counsels their observance.

It should be emphasized again that there is no advantage in putting one's head in the sand and ignoring this as a most unpleasant problem. If there is really no cause for alarm, a qualified person can confirm that happy condition and give couples a doubly welcome assurance. If caution is indicated, steps can be taken to avoid stark tragedy in the lives of prospective parents and unfortunate children who might be born to them. Facing a distressing issue squarely may seem harder than just letting matters slide, but in the long run it is easier.

CHAPTER THIRTEEN

HOW CAN THE QUALITY OF PARENTHOOD
BE KEPT HIGH?

The list of abnormalities believed caused by heredity has been surprisingly reduced by scientific research. Illustrations of this follow:

1. Germinal factors. This refers, for example, to an injury of the reproductive cell before it begins its process of division. Many competent researchers believe it is the cause of a form of feeble-mindedness called *mongoloidism*.

2. Embyronic factors. These come after the reproductive cell starts to divide. It may produce such malfunctions as clubfoot, harelip, cleft palate, and malformed heart. These factors are not inherited but are due to differences in degree of metabolic activity and the presence or absence of certain chemical substances.

3. Fetal factors. These are operative for about seven months before the child is born. These would include nutritional deficiency, hormone disturbances, and infections.

This third group is especially important because it is an area in which something constructive can be done. If parents are neglectful here, they will be responsible for any crippling or handicapping of their children.

This is indicated in a statement made by the Lord to the children of Israel as recorded in Exodus.

> . . . for I the Lord thy God am a jealous God visiting the iniquity of the fathers upon the children unto the third and fourth generation of them that hate me;

And shewing mercy unto thousands of them that
love me, and keep my commandments. (Exodus 20:
5-6.)

Who Are Those Who Hate the Lord?

The Lord has said they are those who do not keep
his commandments. High on the list of those who hate the
Lord are those guilty of unchastity. Unchastity keeps alive
a terrible social disease called syphillis. Despite the fact
that its treatment has been greatly simplified by the development of antibiotics, the rate of its incidence, especially
among young people, has been rising alarmingly. If people
marry who have not been adequately treated for this loath-
some disease, their children may be crippled, deformed or
low in intelligence, or they may suffer other emotional and
character deficiencies.

Tipsy's Story

In the law of health to the Church, the Word of Wisdom, we are counseled to abstain from the use of alcohol.
There is much evidence of the injurious effect on the body
and nervous system of a child born of parents who indulge
in the use of alcohol.

To determine the effect of the use of alcohol on unborn
young, Dr. C. F. Hodge performed a series of experiments
with a little cocker spaniel he called Tipsy. The results indicate how terrible this effect is:

Hodge made her and another dog alcoholic. Of
23 pups obtained from the pair, 8 were deformed, and
9 were dead. Four alone were viable (lived). From a
control pair (non-alcoholic) of dogs, 45 pups were
obtained, of which 4 were deformed, none were born

dead, and 41 were viable. (*Being Well Born*. Michel F. Gyyer. The Bobbs-Merrill Co., Minneapolis, 1927, p. 290.)

A Norwegian Experiment

Doctor Mjoeen cites an interesting parallel between the increase of feeble-mindedness and alcoholics in Norway in a period from 1816 to 1835 when everyone was permitted to distil brandy. In some districts many of the farmers distilled brandy from corn and potatoes, and in such regions during this period, feeble-mindedness increased nearly one hundred percent. Later the home distillation of brandy was stopped. According to Dr. Mjoeen, "The enormous increase in idiots came and went with brandy." (Ibid., p. 28.)

Another Testimony of the Effects of Drugs on the Unborn

First various drugs may pass from mother to embryo. If she smokes or drinks to excess, the nicotine or alcohol in her system may reach the child with harmful, or even disastrous, effects. A large amount of alcohol penetrating to the child may result in its death or malformation. "Monsters" are often supposedly due to such prenatal alcoholization.

If the mother is addicted to the use of morphine or opium to the point where her tissues are saturated with the drug, the child may actually come into the world a drug addict. (*You and Heredity*. Auram Schweitzer. Frederick A. Stokes Co., N.Y., N.Y., p. 35.)

What Is the Effect of Tobacco on Heredity?

Tobacco seems not to be so bad as alcohol, but it, too, has harmful effects on heredity. Tobacco has been given to animals and birds such as guinea pigs, chickens, dogs, and rabbits by various researchers. It was given as a smoke and as a food. Many young were weak and showed evidence of bad effects on various organs of their bodies. Many of them lost the ability to have young.

A striking illustration of the destructive effect of nicotine upon the progeny of tobacco-poisoned mothers was observed by Dr. Kostral, who noted that the infants of women working in a tobacco factory were short-lived. One-third of all their children showed evidence of poisoning of the brain and nerves and died in convulsions.

Such is the terrible story of the relationship between the use of alcohol, tobacco, and drugs, and the stunted, blighted and deformed bodies and minds which result. According to the scripture quoted from Exodus those who use these things and bring these limitations and deficiencies on their children will bring down upon their heads the wrath of God. There is reason to believe that the disobedient may also be required to pay for the blight upon succeeding generations. God's law of justice would imply that such is the case. Certainly no thinking person would want to run the risk of such a righteous judgment.

On the other hand, think of the eternal joy of parents who know their children are as wellborn as possible—who know they have given their children as perfect bodies as possible to help them live happily and successfully, and to fulfil the purpose of their coming into mortality.

What a thrill it would be to have a son declare: "I . . . , having been born of goodly parents," as Nephi wrote of his parents. This tribute is now being read by people in every part of the world even though 2500 years have passed since it was inscribed on the gold plates.

The joy of Lehi and Sariah over this wellborn son and his works will increase throughout eternity. So will that of all parents who leave no stone unturned to provide the best possible heredity and environment for their children. Young couples should aim for this goal and make every effort to achieve it.

How Does Social Heredity Condition the Lives of Children?

The heredity discussed in the preceding section is physical and biological in its nature. There is another aspect of a child's heritage called social heredity. It is often called nurture. There are those who believe it is more important than nature in the formation of personality and character. Nurture is the influence of environment. It is made up in great part of the way families think, act, feel, believe, and live. If a child comes from a home where faith in God is lacking, where educational interests and ideals are low, where recreation consists of drinking, smoking, and physical indulgence, these social habits and attitudes are likely to be passed on to the children. The opposite is also true. Children absorb constantly the wholesome interests, ideals, and habits of their homes. This process goes on subconsciously. As social scientists learn more about human behavior, good and bad, they see more and more evidence of the power of nurture in the child's life.

When you get ready to marry, keep this problem of nurture in mind. Remember that the thinking, believing, and activities of a family are usually strongly ingrained in the children. These children will find it hard to adopt a new orientation toward life. One might say, in a sense, that one marries the family as well as the person. There are cases in which a boy or girl renounces the tastes and interests of a bad home and largely builds his or her own nurture. But these cases are certainly the exception. Don't let love blind you to the importance of a good background in the mate you select.

The other side of this problem is the matter of your own nurture. Into what kind of individual is it turning you? What kind of social heredity are you providing for your children? Much more can be done about social heredity than biological heredity. Scripture indicates that the Lord will hold you responsible in this field of social heredity when you become parents. He has said in the Doctrine and Covenants, "But I have commanded you to bring up your children in light and truth." (D & C 9:40.)

In order to be prepared for this responsibility, you should constantly and actively cultivate the gifts of the spirit. Have faith in God and his plans and purposes for you. Believe that your fellow men are basically good and treat them with kindness and honesty. Develop your talents and power of mind to the greatest possible extent through education. Prepare yourself to make a pleasant, inviting home where your children will grow strong and courageous because of your love, understanding, training, and guidance in their formative years.

What Advantage Do Latter-day Saints Have in Their Biological Group Heredity?

Part of the nature already spoken of is the religious group to which you belong. In a sense this group is an enlarged extension of the family unit. As such it exerts an influence on your personality and character development.

As a group, young men and women of the Church have received a wonderful heredity. This is largely due to the following facts:

1. It took courage and conviction to join the Church in the early days of its restoration.

2. Through bitter persecution the weak-willed and unfaithful were culled—they either left the Church or stayed behind when it moved westward.

3. Only the hardiest survived the rigors or harsh weather, poor food, fatigue, and lack of medical care. Thus an extremely hardy stock remained.

4. The faithful observed the Word of Wisdom and laws of conduct and industry which strengthened their moral and physical fiber.

5. Even though a Latter-day Saint may not be descended from pioneer stock, if either he or his parents are converts and they very likely have a strong group heredity, for even today it takes courage, intelligence, and conviction to join the Church.

Thus most of you have descended from clean, courageous, choice stock. Your progenitors are among the strongest and finest people of history. How blessed you are! In turn if you live faithful and wisely, you may bequeath this same wonderful inheritance to your decendants.

CHAPTER FOURTEEN

HOW IMPORTANT IS GOOD HEALTH
TO MARRIAGE?

John D. Rockefeller, probably one of the wealthiest men of all time, was a virtual invalid at fifty-three. Though he had an income of a million dollars a week, his digestion was so bad he couldn't eat two dollars' worth of food a week. He couldn't sleep or rest. His hair, even his eye-lashes, had fallen out. His skin looked like parchment. People said he was the oldest-looking man they had ever seen. His doctor told him that if a drastic change did not come into his life he could live but a short while. In despair Rockefeller is said to have exclaimed that he would give all the money he had, if he could regain his health and eat normally. It is not uncommon for people who have lost their health to make such a statement. Indeed, good health is basic to the enjoyment of life. Without it life becomes a burden.

This holds true in marriage to an even greater extent. The husband must have good health to meet the keen competition in the world of business and industry. If he cannot hold his job or take care of his business, he will be handicapped in trying to maintain a satisfactory standard of living for his family. Children need a strong, healthy father to be their example and guide as they grow to maturity and independence. It is hard for the father who is ill to fill this role.

The mother in some respects leads an even more strenuous life. She needs good health to give her children strong bodies. The care and nursing of children is a great strain. Doing housework, preparing meals, caring for sick loved ones, helping children through the early years and school years, and training them to be mature, well-adjusted people takes a tremendous amount of energy and physical endurance.

Ill health often breeds irritability and lack of patience. This creates a bad home environment which can have a very negative influence on the development of children into normal adults. Short tempers quickly distort the little molehills of the everyday problems of living into mountains of fiery argument. In contrast, healthy people are more inclined to be patient, good-natured, and optimistic—qualities vital for a happy marriage.

Poor health often means burdensome if not ruinous medical and doctor bills. These expenses in turn limit the ability to have an adequate home and the basic necessities of life. Then money worries may be an additional source of irritability. In some instances the children may be forced to discontinue their schooling too early and be handicapped the rest of their lives.

In addition to their responsibilities to their children, the husband and wife should be able to continue their own religious, cultural, and social activities together. When, through the exhaustion of ill health, they cannot do this, they may undergo a slow, hardly noticeable change in personality. They may lose interest in the uplifting stimulating activities of life. If their talents are not used regularly, they will be lost, and the couple will find nothing to maintain their zest and interest in others. Sometimes ill health turns a happy person into a grouch, a whiner, and a complainer. Such a condition is slow poison to a successful marriage.

There is also the problem of the dangers to others in certain forms of ill health. It is dangerous to associate with people afflicted with certain maladies. Tuberculosis, for example, in an active stage exposes everyone, especially children, to the danger of infection. It seems only sensible and prudent for all young people to have a medical examination to be sure they are equipped, health-wise, to assume the responsibilities of marriage and parenthood. Health examinations are required for many situations less important than marriage. It is difficult to obtain insurance without an examination. Many employers will not hire a prospective employee until they know the condition of his health. If the examination reveals conditions which need attention, care can be given early enough to be effective and less expensive. The young couple can then start life with confidence and a much greater hope of living happily together.

What Is the Lord's Promise for Good Health?

As a Latter-day Saint you have a direct promise from the Lord that if you will live all the teachings of the Word of Wisdom, he will bless your life and marriage with a much greater measure of health. He has made the following promise without condition or exception.

And all saints who remember to keep and do these sayings, walking in obedience to the commandments, shall receive health in their naval and marrow to their bones!

And shall find wisdom and great treasures of knowledge, even hidden treasures;

And shall run and not be weary, and shall walk
and not faint.

And I, the Lord, give unto them a promise, that
the destroying angel shall pass by them, as the children of Israel, and not slay them. (D & C 89:18-21.)

Is There Any Evidence to Support This Promise?

To state the overwhelming evidence for observance
of the Word of Wisdom in all its aspects is beyond the
scope of this study. However, a single study on the smoking of cigarettes is an adequate index for the other facets
of the problem.

Recently some startling statistics were made public
which have a direct bearing on the answer to this question.
Dr. E. Cuyler Hammond, director of statistical research,
American Cancer Society, made the following report.

In answer to the question, "Is smoking a hazard
to health?" the American Cancer Society made a survey of 4,854 recent deaths, all of them white men,
aged 50 through 69. It came up with these statistics:

For all cigarette smokers the death rate runs this much higher than for nonsmokers.

Death from all causes
   63% above nonsmokers
Death from heart disease
   82% above nonsmokers
Death from cancer (all)
   106% above non-
   smokers
Death from lung cancer
   200% above non-
   smokers

For heavy cigarette smokers the death rate runs this much higher than for nonsmokers.
(A pack a day or more)

Death from all causes
   75% above nonsmokers
Death from heart disease
   95% above nonsmokers
Death from cancer (all)
   156% above non-
   smokers
Death from lung cancer
   400% above non-
   smokers

(*Improvement Era*, Oct. 1959)

Could anything be more conclusive? Which road are you traveling? If you are on the wrong road, prepare yourself for the heartache, pain, worry, expense, and discouragement of ill health. Are you willing to shorten your life, and leave hardship and loneliness in the laps of your wife and children merely for the short pleasure you derive?

If you are wise, you will strive to secure for yourself and your family the blessings which good health brings. You will follow the counsel of your Heavenly Father who created your marvelous body. He knows what is best for it and what is harmful to it—just as the engineer knows what is best for a complex piece of machinery, and what substances will ruin it.

Make up your mind to select a mate who has clean habits. Your chances for a happy marriage and healthy children will be multiplied many fold. Yours are the decisions. The results will follow as surely as the day follows the night:

"I, the Lord, am bound when ye do what I say; but when ye do not what I say, ye have no promise."

(D. & C. 82:10.)

CHAPTER FIFTEEN

SHOULD A HUSBAND AND WIFE SHARE RECREATIONAL INTERESTS?

It has been well said that all work and no play makes Jack a dull boy and Jill a dull girl. Play is an important part of the life of young people, and continues to play a role in courtship and marriage. Recreation is most vital in the choice of a mate. It is necessary for a fully successful marriage.

If the term re-creation is used, it is easier to understand the role of play activity in the lives of human beings. The body and the mind are so constituted that they need a change of activities in order to be re-created or brought back to the highest point of efficiency. The office worker who sits all day needs physical exercise to re-establish vigor of muscle. The hard physical laborer, on the other hand, may need mental stimulation. True re-creation, needs to be spontaneous in order to free the mind and body from the fetters of routine. It is therefore something different to almost all people. This makes it difficult to say which type of recreation is best in giving vitality to a marriage. It is a matter for individual consideration.

How Important Is Recreation in Choosing a Mate?

Love has been defined as a highly intensified form of liking. Recreation enjoyed mutually creates a strong feeling of attraction between the participants. The problem then is to determine how much we like people as play-partners during courting and whether or not this feeling is the whole basis of our love-feeling or just a proper share of it.

During courting days the nature of the contact between young men and women is confined almost entirely to play activity. Why is this so? Because courtship is almost entirely a play or leisure-time activity. The ability to dance, swim, play tennis, hike, fish, enjoy concerts, shows, etc., together assumes an importance which is entirely out of proportion. The result is that both boy and girl see in their partners only a "Sunday-best" personality whenever they meet. Little or no attempt is made to meet each other except on social occasions or at times when all the cares and problems of the normal course of life can be pushed out of sight and mind.

After marriage there is a turnabout. Whereas before marriage, social activities were the whole menu, they now become the dessert. And it takes more than dessert to sustain life. It takes more than common recreational interests to find fulfillment in marriage. The many attitudes and skills necessary to build a happy home may not be present even in an elementary form in people who are otherwise "loads" of fun. The high pedestal on which one's mate was situated socially may collapse very suddenly when one has to get down to the business of serious living. The ability to pursue recreational interests should not be over-emphasized. It is an important item in choosing one's life partner, but like certain medicines which are beneficial in proper dosages, it becomes poison if taken in too large amounts.

How Can a Couple Know Whether They Will Find Mutual Joy in Their Recreation?

Since there are almost countless hobbies and activities from which to choose, no recommendations can be made for specific activities. But there are some general principles which will help you work out your own situation.

1. People at the extreme poles of personality types such as introverts and extroverts find it difficult to enjoy the same types of relaxation. A radical difference in tastes such as exists in widely separated personality types will result in stress and strain. This will also be true in other areas of living. Basic differences should give pause for caution and consideration.

2. Some people like active recreation in which they can participate constantly and fully. Others prefer passive recreation—listening and watching. When recreational interests consist wholly of one type or the other there is likely to be difficulty.

3. Some people come from homes where they were taught how to enjoy themselves. Others come from homes where they were not taught, or had no time, or were not allowed to enjoy themselves. Perhaps their lives have been given almost solely to work. Later on in life they may actually have guilt feelings if they engage in recreational activities. It would be well to check how deeply ingrained these attitudes on recreation are. If there is too deep a conviction, it may call for a considerable change in personality. As stated before, this is not easy to achieve.

4. Some people use "escape" recreational activities almost entirely. They do not worry about being with other persons but take their companionship with people of a make-believe world—in movies, TV shows, and magazines or books centering on the bizarre and unreal world of adventure and misadventure. These interests and tastes can and should be detected during courtship. If they go

against the mate's basic recreational needs, trouble lies
ahead.

These then are some of the general principles which
can help you determine whether a satisfying recreational
life is possible with the person you may plan to marry.

Summary

We have now come to the end of this chapter on what
men and women need to bring to a marriage if they are
each to make their required contribution. Some of you may
feel that such a careful consideration of personal traits will
kill romantic feelings. But these traits and qualities are the
very soil in which true love wll grow after marriage. Without them the most romantic pre-marriage feelings between
a young couple are doomed to a crippled existence at the
best. Examining the qualities of character of one's intended
mate may show up the counterfeits of love which blind one
so easily. Avoiding an unfortunate entrapment by counterfeits may prevent a short married life which may end
in hate, in violent ugly emotions, in arguments, perhaps in
divorce, and in some instances in actual bodily harm and
death. True love welcomes the full light of careful consideration. This consideration assures that love will become
longer lasting, sweeter, and more powerful than any feeling based on just one or two aspects of love.

At the beginning of the earth's creation God said,
"Let there be light." Wise couples will apply this to all
phases of their lives. Plans for marriage should begin with
the motto, "Let there be light," on what young people have
to offer each other throughout the eternity they expect to
be together.

Part Four

Why Should You Date?

CHAPTER SIXTEEN
THE PURPOSE OF DATING

In charting the growth of love we note that boys and girls at eleven years of age are usually still interested in each other mainly as friends and schoolmates. They feel little need to respond to each other as members of the opposite sex. As they grow older, a gradual change comes over their play and social activity. Watch a group of these youngsters at play. They are in what might be called the "pushem-pullem-hittem" stage. They tug at each other, slap in play and fun, and push and pull each other around with great gusto. In between, the boys do a few handstands or show off in various other ways. Now and then the little girls gather in groups and whisper to each other, then break out in uncontrolled giggling or in wild gales of laughter.

This is the first stage of a rather long process boys and girls go through in our society in order that they might learn to live acceptably with each other. In simple societies this period is short. Its aims are quickly achieved. In some areas there is absolutely no provision for this phase of growing up; for example, in the Orient all the choosing, accepting, and arranging for marriage is done by the "go-between" who is hired by the parents. The young people may not see or know each other. In fact, they are sometimes engaged to each other by their parents before they are born.

In other countries such as Spain and parts of South America the boys and girls have only a limited association. A chaperone accompanies the young man and woman on each date until they are married. They are never left alone, and very strict rules govern their conduct during this period. Certain cultures, such as some of the South Seas Islands, have tribal rules and taboos which the young people must observe very carefully. If they do not, they may be banished or even put to death. The fact of the matter is the whole tribe enters into the courtship. The prospective bride and groom have absolutely no privacy until they are married.

In our own United States the opposite situation sometimes exists. Young people carry on the activities of dating and courting almost entirely on their own. In certain extreme cases they may not introduce their mate to their parents until after the wedding ceremony. Most young people are wise enough to introduce their friends and dates to their parents at the very first opportunity.

Behind all these customs lies the desire to experience life at its best and fullest, both for the individual and the society to which he belongs. Different cultural groups have various goals and aims in life. As such, they have a high stake in the results of the marriages of their youth. They know happy homes are needed to produce the strong citizens who must conduct the affairs and activities of their community. If the citizens are weak, the nation will be incapable of maintaining itself. The matter of a proper choice of a mate and the rearing of a strong, healthy, well-adjusted family is a prime concern to any nation.

In addition to these considerations Latter-day Saints have a still deeper and more vital concern. They know that only those who have entered into marriage on an eternal basis will have a fulness of joy now and in eternity. A bad choice may, and in some instances does, destroy the possibility of achieving celestial exaltation. It may result in marriage for time only, and inactivity in the Church for the rest of one's life. It may not be possible to rear the children in an effective belief and application of the gospel.

What Is the Best Way to Choose One's Mate?

With so much at stake for everyone individually, and for the nation as a whole, the intelligent, thoughtful person will want to be sure that he uses the best method to choose a mate. Western young men and women object rather definitely to the impersonal way mates are chosen in the Orient. Yet there is food for thought in the fact that such matches are often happier and more successful than the marriages of western people who are free to choose their own marriage partners. The question then arises, is the Oriental way superior, or are westerners failing to use their freedom of choice to the best advantages? Many believe that the latter is true.

Human beings are happiest when they can exercise their free agency and can experience the growth which comes with this privilege. But freedom is not automatically a blessing. Real freedom is not the right to do what one pleases, but the opportunity to do what is best. False freedom is called license. It can create much unhappiness and failure in life. In an attempt to help you use your free agency properly in choosing a mate for your partnership

with God, we shall now discuss dating, courting, and engagement from the standpoint of the ideals of all true Latter-day Saints.

A happy marriage is life's greatest achievement. In
addition to the blessings of children and family, there are
the joys to be experienced by helping one's mate along life's
highway. The ability to experience such joys is acquired
gradually as one practises proper principles and strives to
prepare for marriage. Dating is a vital part of that preparation. It is part of the process of growing up in other
respects. In a simple society only physical growth is important. In our society the mind and emotions must also
be fully developed. Proper dating practices helps one
achieve maturity in this aspect of life.

What Is Dating and What Purposes Does It Serve?

Dating is a very temporary relationship which begins
and ends with each party, dance, or other social function.
There is no further obligation of either partner to the other.
If the young man and young woman are to associate again
socially, the relationship must be re-established by another
request of the boy that the girl again be his companion
for a coming occasion. There is little thought of choosing
a mate or expressing great personal affection. Casual dating might be further defined by setting forth some of its
purposes:

1. Dating allows you, who are quite mature physically, but still need to achieve the other maturities, to associate
together socially until you are ready for marriage.

You are at an age when certain phases of your lives
can and should be carried on together. If you do not have

this limited association, there will be a lack of development which will hinder you in achieving full maturity later on. The normal process of learning to live is divided into various segments such as home, church, recreational and vocational activities. Successful dating experience will help you prepare for all of them.

2. Dating helps you acquire the manners and skills necessary for happy and gracious living.

One of the main reasons some people go from divorce to divorce is that they have not learned that mature love is based on social and spiritual qualities as well as on physical attraction. Physical attraction of itself has a limited function. Used alone, it may serve to satisfy a physical need and perpetuate life. But one who is satisfied with mere physical love is like the person who is satisfied to live in a bare house when he might have a home filled with music and beauty, loveliness and warmth, intelligence and peace, and light and joy! Physical attraction is a part of love, but it must be accompanied by social and spiritual qualities if it is to grow and endure. Yes, temporarily it will do. But how long will it satisfy?

The Savior said, "Man does not live by bread alone." Nothing which is purely physical satisfies very long. The meals you remember most are those which have a social or spiritual quality like birthday parties or Thanksgiving when all the family is together. The food is necessary and good, but the sociability is the enduring part.

So it will be if you have a happy marriage. You will need to know how to live graciously and harmoniously with each other. You will need to practice a form of conduct or etiquette with each other which will smooth over the rough spots and assure your spouse of your feeling of respect, kindness, and affection toward him. This lifts up your mate in his feelings of self-respect and confidence and makes him want to treat you in the same way. Thus are born the feelings of mature love which endure forever and which increase in power and delightfulness as time passes.

Dating provides opportunity to learn to live graciously as a lady or gentleman with all types of personalities under all kinds of conditions. The young person who treats each dating partner with courtesy, and tries to make the date as much fun as possible, even if he does not feel a strong personal attraction, is more likely to be courteous and thoughtful in married life. To read about good etiquette is one thing. To practice it is quite another. What happens when you are discouraged, upset, out of sorts, disappointed, or angered? Such occasions arise frequently in mature life. At such times the deeply ingrained habits of good personality will be worth more than gold to your marital happiness. Dating is a good time to develop thoughtfulness for others, and self-control.

3. Dating permits you to get acquainted with different types of personalities so you can make a wise choice when you are ready for marriage.

Whom will you marry? You may even now have made up your mind to marry a person with certain qualifications; for example, someone with whom a temple marriage is possible. This is fine, but it is distressing to note how often people like yourself, fail to achieve this goal later on in life. Why is this so? One reason might be that you will not have had enough dating experience to properly evaluate the true nature of the individual to whom you are attracted. If you have had adequate, proper dating experience, you will have greater ability to choose wisely.

A second reason for failure to reach this desired goal might be that you have missed or skipped the dating experience and are not successful in stablishing a suitable circle of friends. You may know what kind of person you want to marry, but you may not be able to do this because those who are in your friendship circle are not this type. A group which is too small or is made up of people who are chosen, to a great extent, just because they are "fun" may be able to produce only poor marriage partners. If your list of friends consists mostly of "nonmembers," it is very likely you will pick a non-LDS husband or wife. This is an important matter to consider at the beginning of your dating period.

CHAPTER SEVENTEEN

WHAT STANDARDS SHOULD GUIDE LDS
MEN AND WOMEN ON DATES?

President David O. McKay made the following statements when speaking to about 200,000 young people of the
Church between the ages of 12 and 25.

> A successful marriage begins even before you ap-
> proach the marriage altar. It begins when you are ac-
> cepting invitations in your teenage years to attend
> social parties. It begins with the manner in which you
> say goodnight to your companion. Maintaining an un-
> sullied reputation during courtship contributes to a
> solid foundation upon which to build a happy home.

This quotation highlights the decision which young
people must make at the beginning of their dating activities.
You will remember the Savior went to the wilderness of
Judea after his baptism, to be tempted by Satan. He met
Satan's attempts to get him to misuse his divine powers with
a final decisive *NO*. The reasons Jesus gave were based
on the fact that, although the proposals of the Son of Dark-
ness contained some short-range advantages, they were out
of line with the real purpose of the Savior's earthly mission
and would destroy the possibilities of salvation and exaltation for all men. He realized that one of Satan's favorite
tricks is to confuse the issue so that people cannot see life
in its true perspective.

The New Testament points out another aspect of the
devil's methods: "And when the devil had ended all the
temptation, he departed from him for a season." (Luke

4:13.) Lucifer never gives up. He will be back again and again in your life with new, cunningly disguised approaches, new arguments, new rewards, and new proposals. But no matter what the disguise, Satan's lures can only lead you to misery, sorrow, slavery, destruction, and spiritual death.

Just as Jesus faced his great hour of decision, you too will face yours as you now stand on the threshold of womanhood or manhood. Satan will never let you alone. However, you will be much less subject to his wiles if you will set up without delay a definite standard for your dating activities.

First, you should be aware of the fact that he will try to mislead you in *small* matters. He may whisper that it is all right to go only so far, or that just this once doesn't count. He may then try to destroy the one who has done wrong by suggesting all is lost; that they may as well give up. Young people must see through this deception, and repent, and go on with faith and courage. Satan would like to have you believe sin is always a matter of earth-shaking acts and that little events do not count. The Book of Mormon points out very definitely that he does this to deceive. Nephi describes how Satan will operate in the latter days, the time in which you now live.

> For behold at that day he shall rage in the hearts of men, and stir them up to anger against that which is good.
>
> And others will he pacify; and lull them away with carnal security, that they will say: All is well in Zion! Yea, Zion prospereth, all is well—and thus the devil cheateth their souls, and leadeth them *carefully* away down to hell.   (2 Nephi 28:21-22.)

Satan may directly ask you to do wrong but more than likely he will suggest, rather, that you do something because it is exciting and romantic, as petting is supposed to be. He knows where he is leading you, but he will make sure you don't know. He will try to picture sin as something which is not too bad. He will always try to picture sin without its after effects. Satan will do all he can to mislead you until he has you in his clutch.

Second, you must decide what you will or will not do on your dates and during courting *before* the time comes to make the decision. If as a boy you firmly decide you are going to be a real man and never do, or ask a girl to do, anything which would cheapen or degrade your relationship, you have limited Satan's power over your life. That this is a manly attitude is borne out by the following quotation from the West Point *Manual of Courtesies and Customs of the Service.*

Nothing so quickly discloses the presence or absence of breeding in a man as does his attitude toward women. In polite society a lady's person is inviolate. To touch her except in dancing or other entirely acceptable purposes is inexcusable rudeness.

As a girl you must realize that your body is your most valuable earthly possession. You can either increase or lower its value by your decisions. You can pyramid its value by refusing to give yourself to anyone except a fine, loving companion in temple marriage. You can cheapen the value of your body by using it for questionable popularity, for sensual excitement found in low-grade dates, and for the attentions and gifts of morally filthy men who want to buy you as they would a piece of desirable merchandise.

Remember—you will never have a more priceless treasure than a clean, chaste body.

It should be stressed that the power which draws men and women to each other is wholesome and good when properly channeled. Such affection, in the bonds of a love-filled marriage, makes the difficulties and trials of life more durable. For the proper channeling of the procreative power, our Heavenly Father instituted and sanctified marriage.

> And the Lord God said, It is not good that man should be alone; I will make him an help meet for him...
>
> Therefore shall a man leave his father and his mother, and shall cleave unto his wife; and they shall be one flesh.   (Gen. 2.18, 24.)

Being morally clean is a matter of using one's powers for the best good of the greatest number of people for the longest time. Morality results in joy. Immorality, in bitterness and sorrow.

How Should Petting Be Regarded?

Individuals of wisdom, judgment, and experience in the problems of living say petting is dangerous. Judges, doctors, teachers, church leaders, psychologists, educators, and businessmen are constantly warning young people against expressing their emotions in physical caressing before marriage. It is not that the emotions felt are evil, but that their expression must be reserved for those who have assumed the responsibilities and privileges of marriage.

Very often young people accept the wisdom of this advice but find the pressure of their peer group against them. They face the following pressure-propaganda:

1. Everyone (so some people say) pets.

2. Young people like to be good company. The in- ference is that if young people don't pet, they aren't good company.

3. It makes young people happy to please those to whom they are attracted. Petting seems such an effective and delightful way to do this.

To combat these arguments you need a strength of decision and a long-range view of life which will help you hold a steady course until you have achieved a happy marriage.

What Lies Behind the Desire to Pet?

Psychologists say that habitual petters seek only phys- ical sense enjoyment. Since love's physical impulses lie so close to the surface, they can be quickly and easily aroused. When these smoldering fires of sensual satis- faction are fanned into the bright flame of lust, the intelli- gent choice of a suitable mate becomes very difficult. Phys- ical attraction becomes so powerful that the power of judgment is too weak to consider such important items as harmony of tastes, feelings, beliefs, and temperament. Sheer physical satisfaction requires none of the character and personality needed in true mating. This gratification can be given and experienced by persons who are actually revolting in every other aspect of personality. You will never develop an appreciation of an individual as a desir- able partner in marriage if there is too much emphasis on physical attraction on your dates.

Isn't It Just Plain Natural to Want to Pet?

You have no doubt heard songs which imply that the answer to this question is yes. Certain so-called "experts" in the fields of psychology and sociology affirm this belief. But a little reflection on your part will lead you to the conclusion that this is not so. It has been said that man is the only one of God's creations who can make a choice on *how* he will express his urges and feelings. These "experts" certainly wouldn't approve doing what is natural when it comes to eating. When a dog grabs its food and wolfs it down before some other animal can steal it, it is doing what comes naturally. Because it is a dog it does not worry whether it has to drag its food through the dirt or eat it from an unclean surface. This approach to eating might be called "natural" or animal-like. Compare this with the conditions under which you eat. You strive to make eating a delightful and gracious occasion. Lovely table-cloths, dinnerware, silverware, centerpieces, garnishing and seasoning of food, and serving it at the right temperature, plus congenial sociability at the table have made eating something altogether different from the "natural" approach of animals.

A little thought and study will reveal why this is so in most other areas of living. Our customs and activities in dating, courting, and engagement make them lovely and permanently satisfying because they call for kindness, consideration, and respect toward the object of one's affections. There is a continued attempt to seek favor and acceptance with candy, flowers, entertainment, attention on dates, and the sharing of recreation and social events. That is why courting is such a delightful period in one's life. These activities leave a glow which warms one's marriage forever. In contrast, petting for "kicks," and other sensual indulgence leaves regret which may detract from one's marital happiness. Animal motivation and behavior may seem a natural excuse for petting, but they certainly don't apply to human beings who want to live lives of joy and fulfillment.

You May Never Know Love in Its Fullest Sense if You Pet

When you love someone, you identify yourself with that person. You desire for him all you desire for yourself. You seek his happiness and good. You are happy when he is happy, and sad when he is sad. The habitual petter has no such feelings. He seeks only his own pleasure and uses people to gain that end, just as he uses any object and casts it aside when something else catches his fancy. Sometimes both boys and girls have this attitude. They have neither respect nor love for each other and regard each other as temporary playthings. Because of their short-sightedness, these people are Satan's delight. Such people may become permanently crippled emotionally. The tragedy is that there is often no cure. When they marry, having found what they think is love, they follow a definite downward trail which is as follows: a wedding, an exciting honeymoon, intense physical attraction for each other for a short time, the development of a distaste for each other (as when you have candy for breakfast, lunch, and dinner continuously), and then divorce. This cycle they will probably repeat. They seek emotional satisfaction but cannot find it. Others who have petted habitually may find when they marry that they are unable to find satisfaction. The reason for this is that they have become "fixated." By frittering away their emotional responses in cheap physical indulgence, they become "set." They lose their ability to "stretch" their emotional capacity and to rise to the happiness of mature love. After having played lightly with their physical responses, they find no satisfaction when they need it, just as the boy who shouted "Wolf!" "Wolf" incessantly in fun, failed to get help when he was in earnest. Those who treat lightly the emotional power they possess are doing themselves untold harm. When they meet a person whom they would truly like to love in a permanent and satisfying way, they find to their shock that their emotions do not respond. If you spend your youth climbing molehills of physical satisfaction, you may never be able to climb the mountain of mature love!

What Are the Fruits of Petting?

The Master indicated in Matthew 7:16-21, that there is only one way of deciding the value of anything.

> Ye shall know them by their fruits. Do men gather grapes of thorns, or figs of thistles?

> Even so every good tree bringeth forth good fruit, but a corrupt tree bringest forth evil fruit.

> A good tree cannot bring forth evil fruit, neither can a corrupt tree bring forth good fruit.

> Every tree that bringeth not forth good fruit is hewn down, and cast into the fire.

> Wherefore by their fruits ye shall know them.

Let us then examine the fruits you may expect from petting if you indulge in it extensively.

1. A loss of self-respect. You will come to hate yourself when you recognize the nature of the feelings which caused you to pet.

2. A lifelong remorse over the loss of your most valuable possession—your virtue. If you make a serious moral mistake, no amount of repentance will place you in the position of a virtuous person when you marry and rear your family. Someday your Heavenly Father will remove the bitter cup from your lips if you truly repent, but while you live you will have to take a sip of its dregs from time to time. For murder there is no forgiveness. For adultery, a sin next to murder, there is forgiveness. But it is most difficult to earn because of the nature of the transgression. It might be well to remember the question Joseph of Egypt asked when he was tempted by Potiphar's wife.

". . . how then can I do this wickedness, and sin against God?" (Gen. 39:9.) He most certainly understood how grievous unchastity is in the eyes of God. Do you?

3. Instead of love and respect from those with whom you pet, you will reap hate and distrust when they realize how you have destroyed their character and reputation.

4. A gnawing, sickening fear that if you marry someone else, he will find out what kind of person you were before you married him.

5. You may become the father or mother of a child who will never have the love and affection it deserves, but must go through life knowing it was given away by those who gave it mortal life, to live in an orphanage or foster home, with people who may or may not treat it kindly.

6. You may contract disease, which often takes most painful forms and in some instances, if not treated soon enough and in the proper way, may end in death or insanity. Despite the fact that modern medicine can handle

these diseases more efficiently than ever with antibiotics, there has been a great rise in the venereal disease rate in the past few years. This is especially true of those under 20 years of age. It is well for you to remember that people who are free with their affections may be infected. By their loose morals they have exposed themselves to the scourges which follow unchastity. In turn, they may infect you.

7. Loss of celestial exaltation may be the awful cost of petting. Many people who make serious mistakes in life, for one reason or another, cannot repent. The way of the sinner is truly hard. Because punishment for unrepentant sinners often lies in the future, beyond human sight and knowledge, it seems easier to let things slide. It does not seem urgent to straighten the matter out with the Lord and to pray that mercy replace justice. It is easier— now—to let matters slide. But what of later? Alma has something to say about this.

> For our words will condemn us, yea, all our works will condemn us; we shall not be found spotless: and our thoughts will condemn us; and in this state we shall not dare to look up to our God; and would fain be glad if we could command the rocks and the mountains to fall upon us to hide us from his presence (Alma 12:14.)

These then are the fruits of petting. Are they worth a few moments of excitement?

What Special Problem Does Petting Raise for Girls?

It seems that on girls falls a great obligation of maintaining high standards of conduct on dates if they are to safeguard their reputations and welfare. Whether it is fair or not, girls suffer much more from moral wrongdoing than do the boys. This is due to a number of factors. The following account, based on an actual case history indicates why this is so. Policewoman Kathryn Sullivan tells the story called:

BOYS ALWAYS TELL

One evening a few weeks ago I had just finished addressing the Parents-Teachers association in one of our San Francisco high schools when I was pulled off into a corner by an anxious woman.

"You look worried, Mrs. Howard," I said, "Was it something I said in my talk?"

"Yes and no," she answered, "but I've been doing some thinking. I'm up against a stone wall with Marjorie. She has a blind spot on this petting business. I've pleaded with her on moral grounds, I've tried to talk like a sister, and she has been given the Dutch uncle approach by her father. She says she's smart enough to keep her fingers from getting burned. She's so terribly proud . . . I wish you'd talk to her sometime."

"I will," I said. "On one condition—that I don't pull any punches." She agreed gladly, and a few days later I went to her home for dinner. Marjorie, a nice, bright girl, suspected why I was there, even though I had known the family for several years, because when we were alone later in the evening she said, "All right, Mrs. Sullivan, now you can give me a lecture on petting."

"Not at all, Marjorie. I think you're a fool."

That startled her a little, and I could almost see her defenses stiffen.

"What do you mean by that?" she asked resentfully.

"You're a fool," I repeated calmly, "because boys always tell." Marjorie looked at me for a moment then grinned.

"Well," she said, "that's a new approach."

"You know Patty Blane, don't you?" I went on, ignoring her jauntiness. Marjorie nodded.

"Last Saturday night she sat in the back seat of a car at the beach with Eddie Smith for two hours. Last Wednesday she was petting with another boy in the Roof Garden of the Forest Hotel. The week before—"

"Oh-h . . . I see," Marjorie interrupted angrily. "The police spy squad is out again."

"No, Marjorie," I said slowly. "The boys talked themselves. They always talk. Eddie tells Bill, and Bill tells Jack and you girls are just verbal footballs for their boasting."

She was thoughtful for a moment, but she wasn't going to be sold so readily. "Maybe they do talk," she said uneasily, "but it's only about girls like Jackie Brown. She necks with everybody."

"How do you know?"

"Well, . . . uh . . . because everybody says so," she said weakly.

"That's just it, Marjorie. I knew Jackie Brown when she first went to your school. She was just as pretty and just as nice as you are. And then some boy talked about her, and she got a lot of dates. The boys talked one after another. They've done such a good job, she's been talked right out of school. And pretty soon," I continued, "they'll be talking about what you did at Ted Johnson's party last week."

"They can't. No one saw me!" she blurted. Then as the significance of my remark dawned on her, Marjorie suddenly burst into tears and ran up to her room.

It was drastic treatment, perhaps, but I had touched a vulnerable spot, and she would remember the sting of it for a long time.

But since the first time a parents' group asked me to talk frankly to their daughters about petting, I have drummed at their pride with that one thought: "Boys always tell." I've found that boys from sixteen to sixty can't resist the urge of bragging. And finally, because I have seen some tragic results of wagging tongues, I have accepted invitations to talk against petting.

In my relationships with girls, both in and out of the juvenile court, I have discovered that many yielded to rash impulses the first time only after the boys promised: "You're the only one I've ever been with," or "I won't tell anybody," or "We'll keep this our own little secret." In 98% of the cases, the girls learned to their shames that the boys have "told."

I'd rather have a girl dance all night than take an hour's automobile drive on a dark road. For I know that when petting starts, gossip is only a step behind, and enough idle talk will leave a scar that doesn't heal without heartaches. I've learned, too, that when girls get into a jam, most boys claim: "Well, you can't prove I'm the one," or "I wasn't the only one who went with her." And the harsh truth is that you can't prove it, in seven cases out of ten.

Why do "boys always tell?"

It's quite simple. It's human nature to boast. It gives the boys a sense of conquest, and they put girls in the same class with their other accomplishments. Just keep that in mind, girls, the next time you're tempted to pet—or worse. Boys always tell! (*Your Life*. Kathryn Sullivan (No. & Vol. unknown). pp. 49-52, copyright 1941.)

"... and then ..."

CHAPTER EIGHTEEN

WHAT MAKES A GOOD DATE?

Now that you know that dates are a most important phase of your preparation for marriage, and that making petting a part of them does not bring happiness, you will want to discuss the positive aspects of dating: how to ask for a date, how to prepare for it, and what to do while you are on a date.

How Do You Ask for a Date?

This is a soul-shaking experience for many boys who would rather face a hard-hitting opponent on the football field than ask a slip of a girl for her companionship for an evening. Of course, it is wholly in the boy's mind. Even if the girl wanted to do so, she couldn't hurt him . . . physically. The boy is afraid because he is fearful that he won't measure up, that his tongue will suddenly cease functioning, that he will be unable to find the right words, or that the girl may turn him down, etc. Truly, in this instance, the coward will die a thousand deaths. If boys will follow a simple little format, the problem may not be solved but it will be held down to a workable size. This approach for asking for a date is somewhat as follows:

If it is on the telephone the boy should:

1. State his full name. "This is John Smith," then,

2. *Do not* ask the girl what she is doing Friday night, but say: "If you are free Friday night, would you go with me to the Senior Hop?" No more, no less. Then she can

say yes or no, knowing full well what you are inviting her to *before* she has to make a decision. Thus the boy does not get a guarded or evasive answer or even a "turn-down."

3. Every girl worth knowing and asking for a date will be as kind and courteous as she can. If she already has a date, she can thank the boy for asking her. If she would like to date the boy in the future, she might encourage him to call her on another occasion. Even if she declines, she should do so with appreciation.

4. Every boy should realize it is perfectly proper for a girl to decline a date which does not appeal to her without having her decision to do so cast any reflection on him. People are all different, and they have different goals in life. Until you are well-acquainted with a person you do not know what these are. As a boy you should accept the possibility that a girl may, with perfect honesty, decline a date for any reason which seems sufficient to her, without having to discuss that reason with you. This should not prevent you from asking another girl. Don't you, in fact, do the same thing by choosing to ask Sally and not Jane instead?

5. You should not wait until the last moment to ask a girl and then feel bad if she already has a date. You should make your wishes known as soon as practicable. You will avoid disappointment for yourself and embarrassment for the girl.

When Does a Good Date Begin?

Whether you will have a good time on your dates depends on how you have lived and do live in everyday life. On dates you begin to sense how important your personality and attitudes will be later on when you marry. There are certain attitudes you should cultivate as much as possible so they will be second nature when you go on dates. Some of these are:

1. Be sincere and genuine in what you say and do. Sincere people give others a sense of security and well-being.

2. Be actively concerned about the happiness and welfare of other people. Be constantly on the alert to be helpful in the little matters which can mean so much to those around you.

3. Support the activities of others. Don't try to advance your own interests and desires too much. Be modest in noting your achievements and help promote the ego-status of others.

4. Try to cultivate interest in many facets of life so you can talk and associate with people from many walks of life in their activities.

5. Smile. A smile is the key to the hearts of most people. It is the mark of a good personality and is so accepted by most people. Recently a large group of young men were shown the pictures of 140 girls and were asked to indicate which ones they liked. When all the reasons for their choices had been counted, it was found that one thing characterized the pictures chosen most often. There was a smile on the face of the girl. The researcher who made the study said there was no doubt that the ability to smile was the most important single element in the popularity of people.

JUST A SMILE

It costs nothing—but creates much.

It enriches those who receive it, without impoverishing those who give it. It happens in a flash, and the memory sometimes lasts forever. It creates happiness in the home, fosters good-will in business, and is the countersign of a friend. It is rest to the weary, daylight to the discouraged, sunshine to the sad, and the best antidote for trouble. It cannot be bought, begged, borrowed, or stolen, for it is something that is of no earthly use to anyone until it is given away. And if in the hurried rush of business you meet someone who is too weary to give you a smile . . . leave one of yours. For no one needs a smile quite as much as he who has none left to give.

—Author unknown

How Can I Be Popular?

The big question, in the mind of every boy or girl is, what will my partner think of me? If you will try to put into practice the five preceding suggestions on each and every date, you will generally have reason to be happy with the answer to that all-important question.

Of course, every date begins with your preparations for it, before you step outside your own home. Presentable people command respect. With clothes suitable for the occasion and reflecting modesty and good taste, you will feel assured and self-confident.

Many lists have been made up of what boys like in girls on dates and vice versa.

The following one might be called "How to Be Popular."

BOYS AND GIRLS

1. Let the kids you are with know you like them.

2. Don't monopolize the conversation.

3. Be yourself at all times. Don't be two-faced.

4. Be clean in dress and grooming.

5. Don't become a twosome hermit. Even if you are going steady, continue to see your other friends, and dance with them.

6. If you were going steady but suddenly broke up, don't go around cutting down your former date.

7. Be friendly. Smile at people even if you don't have a reason to.

8. Think of ways to make others feel important.

9. Don't chew gum on dates.

10. Don't blow bubble gum.

11. Don't crack your knuckles.

12. Don't pet just because you're too dull to have anything else to do.

13. Don't be a leech.

14. Don't make a great show of your superiority even if you know you're superior.

15. Don't lend money too easily.

16. Don't be a night owl—it produces circles under your eyes and zeros on your exams.

17. Keep attending games even when your team is losing.

18. Don't boo the umpire or referee.

19. Don't always take snap courses.

20. Don't be a teacher-polisher, but do be a good classroom citizen.

21. Have friends from other schools.

22. Show appreciation for presents even if you had hoped for something else.

23. Don't spend too much on your girl friend or boy friend when buying a present.

24. Keep your fingernails trimmed and clean.

25. Don't drink. Don't smoke.

26. Don't take foolish dares.

27. Shake hands *firmly* with people when you are being introduced.

28. Find out beforehand what your date is going to be wearing on special occasions and dress accordingly.

29. Think up unusual parties like going to the county fair, or picnicking after swimming, or having a hobo party.

30. Don't exclude someone from a social group because of prejudice.

31. Learn to write legibly.

32. Even if you're not as popular as you'd like to be, don't be a bookworm.

33. Don't use big words unless you know what they mean.

34. Use clean speech.

ESPECIALLY FOR GIRLS

1. On a date don't yak all the time.

2. Ask your boy friend's mother if you can help her.

3. Be attentive. Thank your date for his courtesies.

4. Don't wear clothing that is too tight.

5. Don't invite your boy friends over without permission if you are baby sitting.

6. Don't go on crazy fad diets.

7. Don't brag about your date last night.

8. Learn to use "make-up" properly.

9. Remember your date really wants you to be a lady.

ESPECIALLY FOR BOYS

1. Treat your date with courtesy; it will make her feel "special."

2. Try to talk about things girls are interested in once in a while.

3. Practice your good manners on every date, no matter if it is a disappointing one.

4. Once you make a date, don't break it.

5. Be on time.

6. Make the acquaintance of your date's family before you leave to go on your date.

7. Always walk on the outside when you are walking down the street.

8. Ladies first:
>When you are introducing people
>Sitting down at a table
>Getting into an automobile
>Going into a theater behind an usher
>Entering and leaving a restaurant
>Going through doors

You go first:
At the theater, if there are no ushers
Down any dark and narrow hall or alley, or path
Into buses (so you can pay the fare and guard
   against people pushing her around
Up ladders, steep steps, etc.

9. Open car doors, etc., for your date.

10. Don't smoke. Don't drink.

11. Don't swear, use profane or vulgar language.

12. Don't give your date a line. She will probably suspect (rightly so) that you give it to all the girls.

13. Don't let your heart run away with your ballpoint. Old notes and love letters can sound awfully silly.

14. If your date has been asked to be home at a certain time, see to it that she gets there without fail.

15. Drive carefully. Your date has a value beyond price to many people. The fact that you don't value your own life and have to build up your ego by being a silly and dangerous driver doesn't reassure them. Girls like maturity, the grown-up approach, not show-off kids.

Now that you have gone through this list, how do you rate? Where are your weak spots? What do you need to develop to be popular? What else would you suggest?

CHAPTER NINETEEN
HOW DO YOU PLAN A GOOD DATE?

No person is very successful who does not know how to plan. Our earth with all that it contains, was planned and created spiritually before it was actually created physically. The architect prepares blueprints of his buildings. The engineer creates his bridges and roads on paper before a bid can be made or a shovel of dirt can be turned. Before a doctor performs a difficult piece of surgery, he goes through it step by step in his mind, reading and refreshing his memory if necessary. The nurses have all the instruments and supplies on hand and arranged in perfect order before the operation begins. Nothing which can be planned is left to chance. Check, and you will find that planning precedes the activities of most successful people. It goes without saying that this would also apply to dating activities. The following standards will help you to plan your dates and make them satisfying occasions which will contribute to your development and chances for a happy marriage.

What Are the Advantages of Group Dating?

Your early dating experience should be on a "group" basis. If you are bashful, it will help to be with others who are also on their first dates. If it is hard for you to carry on an interesting conversation, you won't be embarrassed. If there are several in the party, they can all offer their comments and prevent the painful pauses which occur when two people are alone. After a period of group dating you will feel freer and more at ease when you are alone. You can watch others and learn how to conduct yourself better. When there are several in a dating group it is possible to carry on more activities and have more fun than if you are alone. There is moral strength in being with others. You are not so likely to have your attention focused on yourself, and you will be less inclined to resort to petting and physical familiarity.

What Type of Activities Are Most Fun on Dates?

Experience indicates dates turn out best when young people expend much physical energy together. If this is to be so, they should engage in "large-muscle" activities. Examples of these are: hiking, dancing, softball, skiing, skating, bicycling, etc. Any activity where you can play hard until you are thoroughly tired and relaxed is acceptable. Your planning for your dates should include as many activities of this type as possible. Another advantage is that being with others increases the fun.

Where Should You Go on Your Dates?

It is easy to get lost if you go into strange territory. People also get lost morally and spiritually when they wander into unfamiliar places where they are not known. You have no doubt noticed that you are reminded of your ideals most strongly when you are around your parents, friends, home, or church. If you go to secluded areas or into unfrequented places of entertainment, you may tend to lose your sense of moral direction. It may then seem right to do things of which you will later be ashamed. Going "slumming" may lead you into pastimes you will

"Choose ye this day . . ."

regret when you get back with your loved ones and regain your sense of right and wrong. As the hunter is
careful not to get lost, so you should be careful to stay on
safe, familiar ground as to the places you go and the persons you date.

Should You Go to Satan's Meetinghouses?

President Brigham Young made the statement that
Satan and his hosts hold conferences when the Saints do
and that they too plan their activities. What would be more
logical than to believe the devil has his meetinghouses and
recreation centers? He would like to have you come there
so he can ensnare you more quickly and permanently.
Satan's meetinghouses are easy to recognize, but sometimes
young people in ignorance or in search of fun frequent these
resorts. These are run by unscrupulous people who may actually cater openly and skillfully to people who desire
drunken, lewd, and immoral conduct. Roadhouses, beer
taverns, and cheap public dance halls are most guilty of
this. Sometimes, however, these dens of iniquity are very
"plushy." But cocktail bars with beautiful carpeting, drap-
ery, lighting, and mirroring do nothing to change the effect
of the alcohol consumed there, or to elevate the activities
people pursue there in the name of entertainment. When
you step into such environs, you are on Satan's side of the
fence. Dates at such places frequently end in shame and
sorrow. If you are wise, you will never go to one of the
devil's recreation halls. You will tell your date "I just
don't enjoy this place. Please take me home."

Have you ever seen a river which lacked a definite
channel and wandered all over the valley floor? Have you
noticed how dirty the water is in such cases? It does not

offer the fisherman any sport, for there are no fish in it. Have you noted that its banks are not lined with refreshing trees and shrubbery? Were you aware that its waters could not be contained in a dam so the desert could be irrigated?

If the electricity in your home fails, you are greatly handicapped. You are without heat, light, refrigeration, or entertainment. As useful as this source of energy is when brought in at a price with wires, you would not want it as a gift if it came in as lightning, would you? Lightning is uncontrolled, violent, and out of hand. In the same sense all elements of our personal lives are useful only when they are under control and serving definite purposes.

It is so with human emotions—especially when there is a possibility of a strong reaction. Dating may be a fertile situation for trouble if you do not channel your emotions into definite, planned activities. You should plan to keep busy. It is when people just sit with nothing to do that trouble starts. Their energies become destructive as they wander beyond proper bounds. You will find it desirable to keep busy on your dates. Listen to the radio, play records, dance, view your slides or picture album, discuss a book, school assemblies, the operetta, the yearbook, the Junior Prom, the next football or basketball game, or any other topic of mutual interest. Have some games to play. Moving water doesn't stagnate and become filthy. Neither does an active, controlled mind. If you haven't anything definite and interesting to do, you will probably be wise to end your date as soon as possible.

Does Satan Rule the Hours After Midnight?

An outstanding physician of the State of Utah once said he could not recall having had to counsel any young people who were in trouble who had not made their mistake *after midnight*. He didn't say anything about Satan, but he did point out several facts. He said when people stay up late and don't get enough sleep, the human body loses its ability to function. The mind becomes dull. The powers of reason fade out very rapidly. As the evening's entertainment is generally over, likely as not there is nothing to do but talk—or pet. The writer served as a bishop of a large ward for ten years. During that time he had to listen to stories of sorrow and woe from *good* young people who had been unwise in their conduct. In their tearful confessions, they bore the same testimony time and time again.

"It was near morning."

"We stayed out alone too much after midnight."

"I don't know why we did it. We didn't intend to. We are terribly ashamed. It seemed we were so tired we couldn't think."

Is this one of the reasons our Heavenly Father placed the following admonitions in the Doctrine and Covenants?

> Cease to be idle, cease to be unclean, cease to find fault with one another; cease to sleep longer than is needful. *Retire to thy bed early,* that ye may not be weary, arise early, that your bodies and minds may be invigorated. (D&C 88:124.)

If this counsel is heeded, it would help eliminate parking and petting on "lover's lane," or the front porch, or alone in the living room. Set an early hour to end your date and abide by that decision. Say good night and mean it—and keep it a *good* night.

Who Should Plan a Date?

Some dates need only a minimum of planning. But even when young people know each other well their dates should be planned. When will the date begin? With whom are they going? Will there be some refreshments afterward? If it is a formal dance and the boy wishes to give a corsage to the girl, he should find out what color her dress will be so the corsage will be appropriate. The date will be much more fun if this planning is carried on together.

There are other dates where almost all the activities for the evening need to be planned. It has been said that anticipation is more fun than realization. Have you ever noticed how much fun it is to plan and to look forward to an event? If you have not been planning your dates with your prospective partner, you have missed a vital and most rewarding part of your social life.

Girls rate good planning by boys high on their list of courtesies. They prefer boys who find out things ahead of time—how much tickets cost, how to introduce people to each other, how to enter a movie theatre or a restaurant. All these little courtesies make a very favorable impression on a girl.

Who Sets the Standards for a Date?

Have you ever thought that question through carefully? Do you know what you should do? Do you do it? If not, why not? Where did you get your standards? How well will the results of these standards serve you 20-40-60 years from now?

People of the world generally feel that it is woman who gives beauty, strength of character, and spirituality to life more often than man. The Church of Jesus Christ of Latter-day Saints does not recognize a double standard. It teaches there is only one standard, chastity, for men and for women. Some boys do not realize they can lose their chastity piecemeal, so they decide to pet a little for excitement's sake. In such cases, you girls will have to set the standards at the outset of your dates. You should not let things get started before you indicate to the boy his conduct is not acceptable to you. This can and should be done without insulting him. You should *pleasantly* and *firmly* let him know where you stand. You must remain firm and not compromise even if the boy *seems* angry or insulted — for he might act that way for a while. If he continues sulking and no longer desires to date you, do not feel bad. He does not have the character and personality you want in a dating partner. But you will be happily surprised to note how a girl rises in the esteem of a *real* man when she indicates she does not hold herself or her emotions cheaply.

A certain very popular girl set the standard for her dates in the following manner. When the boys wanted to pet, she did not respond to their advances. Pretty soon the boys became tired and quit. She then put forth every effort to help him really enjoy the activities of the evening. THIS IS IMPORTANT! She replaced the harmful with the helpful. This girl became so popular she couldn't accept nearly all the dates she was offered. She later chose from among several fine young men her mate for all eternity. She was climbing the mountain, not all the molehills.

Are You a "Contrectative" Girl?

Does that word throw you? You can't be blamed. It isn't used very often. It is a technical word employed by psychologists. It means a strong desire to feel, to touch, and to experience and be part of the outside world by physical contact. Have you ever watched how babies touch and rub things and then put them in their mouths. They are highly contrectative—and so are girls and their mothers. Have you ever watched ladies as they feel the fabric in a store? Or observed how they love to rub and pat little babies or soothe the foreheads of their children when they are sick? No doubt you have had the comfort of your mother's gentle hand on your brow when you were feverish and ill. Do you remember how the hurt went out of your bumps when Mother rubbed them? God made mothers and girls contrectative for a purpose. But the possession of that power and urge can also create a problem for you girls. It causes you to like to touch your date, to play with his tie, pull on his coat lapels, smooth down his hair, rub the back of his neck and sit close—oh, so close to him— in a car. Girls don't mean it to be so, but sometimes boys misinterpret such actions. They feel it is an attempt to "lead them on." Girls are shocked when the boys become disrespectful. It is well for you girls to remember that boys are constituted differently from you. Their temptations are greater. Girls can be helpful by recognizing this condition and by not being too familiar. Familiarity breeds contempt. There are many ways a girl can let a boy know she likes him without making it difficult for him to act like a gentleman. If he is a red-blooded man, he will know that he has to be careful, and he will greatly admire and respect you if you will help him. Won't you, by not being too contrectative, help your dates be the man they would like to be and must be if they are to be good husbands and fathers?

What Should Be the Center of Interest on a Date?

It seems desirable to put oneself at the center point of interest because one wants to be accepted and appreciated. But here you have a practical application of the statement that he who loses his life will find it. If you can forget about yourself, your hopes and fears, and help your partner enjoy the *activities* of the evening, your interests will be taken care of in the best possible way. It has been said that activities of the right kind are like proper clothing. Both bring out the high lights of one's personality. You have perhaps met men and women whose clothes were so flashy and unusual that they literally smothered any individuality their wearers might have had. They were so colorful that the people who wore them seemed to be colorless. Strong individuals wear clothes which supplement their personalities instead of submerging them. Drawing attention to one's personal charms instead of putting these qualities into one's activities is like wearing clothes which drown out the effect of one's total personality. You will never appear in a better light to others than when you forget yourself for the sake of making the party or dance a delightful success for your date.

Why Is Wine a Serpent, and Strong Drink a Mocker?

Very few of you could be induced to carry a rattlesnake around in your purses or pockets could you? Why? Because it would be too dangerous, you say. You can never tell when it would bite you. But too many young people are willing to take another serpent, wine or strong drink the Bible calls it, on dates with them. This serpent is much more dangerous than a copperhead or a coral snake. Such snakes can only kill the body at the worst. Strong drink can and does, day in and day out, poison the soul. We all shudder in horror when the newspapers or radio reports a plane crash in which people were mangled and cut, some spending months in hospitals only to remain cripples for the rest of their natural lives, while most were killed out right. But nothing is ever said of those numerous souls which suffer spiritual death by having made wrong decisions while their sense of reason was befogged with alcohol. These lives are blighted by immorality, an immorality made possible because minds, in an alcoholic stupor could not tell right from wrong, good from bad. As you would not accompany an individual on a date who carries a live rattlesnake with its fangs bared, so you should not accompany a person who wants to make alcoholic drinks part of any date. Young people who encourage the use of alcohol on dates seek to lower the sense of reason and judgment in themselves and their partners. They want a release of the moral brakes. They want to eliminate resistance. They want you to forget your own best interests and give in to them. They want to take advantage of you even if it destroys your character, your reputation, and your future. The use of alcohol, or any other narcotic, is an open invitation to degradation and shame. No boy or girl who has any consideration for his or her future happiness will ever permit alcohol to have any part on a date.

Am I More Tempted Than Other People?

Sometimes you may feel that other people are not tempted as sorely as you to do things they know they shouldn't. If you had the opportunity to become intimately acquainted with other people's lives, you would find this is not so. All people are subject to Satan's temptations. The greater one's possibilities the harder Satan will work on that individual. The Savior had to fight an "all-out" battle with Satan for forty days. Even then, as you learned before, the devil departed only for a season.

Satan will strike at you more often, strongly and quickly, through your power to be a co-creator with your Heavenly Father than in any other way. Why? Because a mistake here brings the greatest possible destruction. It is the fountainhead of life, the beginning of glory and exaltation. Satan likes to strike in a manner which will have the greatest overall effect. If some of you bowl, you will be aware of the effect of a properly spun ball. No bowling ball, no matter how skillfully it is thrown, can knock down all the pins for a strike. But if the ball is thrown in the right way at the proper pins, it will set up a chain reaction which will bring all the other pins down, and you have a strike. This set-up Satan will try with you. Have you ever stopped to figure out how long-lasting the effect of immorality is, how many people it effects, how much joy and happiness it destroys? If murder is a strike in Satan's game, immorality brings down nine pins.

Are Clothes Important for Good Dates?

People who do not have self-respect find it most difficult to obtain respect and consideration from others. One of the strongest evidences of self-respect is the manner in which people clothe their bodies. Clothes may be most effective in creating the "tone" of a festive occasion. Our nicest dances are "formal." We have "Sunday-best" clothes. Certain recreational places, like roller-skating rinks, insist that "Levis" are out of order. Dress slacks seem to create a more refined atmosphere so that "rough housing" seems out of place.

Most male fashions seem to call for the boy to be properly clothed. But it seems that female dress, as conceived by the people of the world, is all too often based on the idea that the womanly form is most charming when exposed. Elder Hugh B. Brown points out how seriously the matter of following immodest fads of dressing affects the lives of young women.

We wonder if our girls know what kind of females they imitate when they immodestly expose their bodies to public view because it may be fashionable. They should know of the lewd, sinister, and sensuous designs of such females in these disgusting displays. If they knew the source of some modern fashions, no sensible, self-respecting girls would mimic their authors or risk the implications and deductions of immodest exposure and conduct.

Also, if young women knew how good men, young and old, react to such exposures, we doubt if they would be so foolish and naive. The immodest revealing of the female form causes the lewd to leer and lust, decent men to blush and protest, while fathers and brothers are embarrassed, offended, and alarmed. Even lewd men have a certain disgust for nude women.

The exposing of the uncovered body (male or female) (Italics author's) to public view is like a for sale notice indicating cheap, shop worn, or marked down goods. In a mercantile establishment, such merchandise generally invites handling and is cheapened and soiled thereby.

Decent men looking for wives and choosing mothers for their children, reject girls who make a public display of their bodies. They want wives who will become examples to their own daughters, and they know immodesty is the first step toward unchastity. (*Improvement Era*. Hugh B. Brown. Nov. 1959, p. 821.)

Boys sometimes dress immodestly by wearing their slacks or trousers so low it is nothing but vulgar. Occasionally a boy thinks it is smart to leave his shirt unbuttoned so that his manly (?) bosom is revealed.

Both boys and girls are sometimes immodest by the kind of profane, obscene language they use. Their stories are dirtier than the inside of a chimney. Their whole vocabulary reveals a soiled mind and emotions full of foul ulcers of lust and sinful thinking.

Immodesty of dress, speech, or actions has no place in the dating scheme of a respectable Latter-day Saint boy or girl.

If you will observe as many as possible of these suggestions for carrying out your dates, the next few years can be one of the happiest and most fruitful periods in your life. It will be profitable to follow the Savior's admonition, "to watch and pray always, lest ye fall into temptation." This means two things (1) that you ask your Heavenly Father to bless you on your dates and (2) that you never do anything on a date for which you would not ask his permission or about which you would not be happy to have him know.

It may help to remember that you are never so far away from home, nor is any night so dark, nor any road

so secluded that what you do is not as evident to your
Heavenly Father as if it were done in the middle of Times
Square in the brightness of the noonday sun.

You know you are among God's choicest spirit children and that while you cannot picture it fully now, a great
destiny, an eternity of joys lies ahead of you. No one has
greater reason to respect himself or herself and others than
you have. With this sense of self-esteem and confidence in
your own future you will find it easier to treat others with
respect, trying always to help them grow in personality and
character, so they too can realize the purpose for which all
of us came to earth.

CHAPTER TWENTY

FOR GIRLS ONLY

Junior high and senior high school girls are well aware of the fact that not a few of their number will have rather infrequent dating opportunities. Some go through this period in their lives without any dates at all. Under such conditions it is easy to become discouraged and to feel there must be something basically wrong with one's personality. However, a closer look at the matter will reveal that this is not necessarily so.

First, boys are often several years behind girls in social development at this time in life. Dating simply does not seem as important in their lives as it does in the lives of the young ladies. They find adventure, excitement, and fulfillment in such activities as hunting, fishing, and competitive sports. There is little sense of failure, of being left out, or neglected if they are not part of the social whirl. The result is that girls, to whom dancing and party participation are very important, are not going to have enough escorts. At this age many boys are shy and do not feel at ease on a date. They are not sure they will be able to act properly in a social situation. Some feel awkward on a dance floor. Others are almost tongue-tied when they are around members of the opposite sex. Dates are generally expensive, and boys may feel they cannot afford too many of them.

At this time of life boys are sometimes not interested in the quality of the personality and character of a girl as much as they are in having a girl who is "fun." Unfortunately this "fun" is all too often an unreserved willingness to pet and neck. Fortunately, the average young lady is reserved. She does not want to be handled and fondled just to provide some boy with physical thrills. This is as it should be. She may be limiting the dates available in high school by such a reaction, but she should certainly not feel bad about it. Boys do not respect girls who are too free with their personal favors. They look upon them as objects of conquest, as interesting diversions. At this time in life young men and women may have different points of view on the purpose and activities of dating. When the boys grow up and become interested in marriage, their points of view change. They no longer seek a girl just to have "fun." When seeking a mate, the mother of their children, they are looking for a girl who has reserved herself for just such an opportunity. The girl who was popular in high school because she was too unrestrained on her dates may find she is now almost forgotten. The wise girl will know this and remember it when she feels disappointed and frustrated in her early teens. It will help her to plan for a permanently satisfying future rather than throwing herself away spiritually and emotionally in exchange for a few years of excitement in high school.

"Then Don't Stand Idly Looking On"

These words from the popular hymn certainly have a direct application here. A lack of dates may close some doors in your life, but it will certainly open others. In order to help you open them a few suggestions follow:

1. *Develop Your Talents.* Music, speech, drama, and

art offer many fields for the development of personal talents. The blessings derived from such training are great and eternal. This is especially true if they are used for the blessing and benefit of others. Their development and use also provides many contacts with young men which will be most satisfying and wholesome.

2. *Develop an Interest in Other People and in Activities Which Are Not Wholly Personal.* If there is anything which helps guarantee strong character and personality development, it is this. Help your school have a successful student government or extracurricular program. Work on committees, run for an office, help others run for office, build floats, join a cheering section, help with the school paper and yearbook. It doesn't matter too much what you do as long as you enter into it wholeheartedly and *for the benefit of your school.*

Watch for opportunities to encourage and assist people who are less fortunate than you are. It may be a matter of a smile, a cheery hello, a statement of appreciation, or taking the time and trouble to congratulate someone who isn't necessarily important to you. Make a visit to the housebound and bring them a meal, read to them, or provide them with some informal entertainment. They can give you nothing but heartfelt appreciation, but such service will help you develop interest in others. This "turning-out" of one's life orientation creates charm and poise and is a quality which is so rare in this self-centered world that it makes the person who possesses it very attractive.

3. *Master as Much as Possible the Complex Skills of Managing a Home and Mothering Children.* You may well realize that almost any career a woman may follow will be

simpler than that of being a wife and mother. That is why this calling which God gave you is so soul-satisfying. It fills great, deep, and eternal spiritual and emotional needs. Naturally, meeting the requirements of this calling *is not easy*. So the more adequately you are prepared, the easier the task will be when it comes, and the deeper will be your personal satisfaction.

Some young men sense quickly whether a girl knows how to conduct a household economically, pleasantly, and attractively. Whether a girl can cook is important. The trite cliche', the way to a man's heart is through his stomach has a lot of truth in it. A girl is wise to let the young man sample the results of her cooking skill.

Fathers love their children and are much concerned about them even though they have to be away from home all day. It is reassuring to them to know that their wives are capable of taking good care of the family while they are out in the world earning a livelihood. Through formal training in high school and college and by working with and learning from her own mother, the young woman can prepare herself for these responsibilities.

4. *Promote Mixed Group Activities.* As was indicated in the section on dating, group dating is an easy, natural way to initiate one's social life. Girls can more properly take a measure of initiative in this form of activity than they can in individual dating. They can co-operate with other girls in planning group activities in which boys may participate without going through the procedure of choosing a partner specifically for an evening's activities. Firesides, Mutual activities, ward and stake activities provide a regular and ready made schedule for such occasions. If

"Say, these are good!"

you want to increase your true popularity, support these with your wholehearted interest, effort, and enthusiasm. This should be done with the goal of helping others uppermost in mind, not merely as a matter of having fun.

5. *Make Yourself as Physically Presentable as Possible.* This does not mean you need to become a clotheshorse. But the styles you choose should accentuate your good points and tone down your bad ones. It might be helpful to have a teacher, your friends, a beautician, or anyone whom you feel is competent, evaluate your hairstyling, use of cosmetics, choice of clothing styles, your manner of walking and speaking. Above all else, do not give these items undue attention. Do not try to be perfect. Be yourself, don't try to imitate others. After you have adjusted as well as you can, concentrate on making others happy and at ease.

Watch your diet and your weight. Frustrated people have a strong tendency to compensate by overeating. Avoid the excessive use of sweets, oils, fats, too many starches and carbohydrates. Create a picture in your mind of the physical appearance you desire, then eat, exercise, and live to achieve it. Avoid "crash diets," going without meals, and food faddism. Eat normal, adequate, and healthful foods at every meal. Learn how many calories you need for a trim figure and obtain these from wholesome, natural foods. A nice physical appearance encourages and sustains a happy, contented state of mind.

6. *Strengthen Your Faith—Improve Your Outlook on Life.* People who have a strong faith in God and believe that life is purposeful are inclined to be more cheerful and optimistic than those who lack faith. Try to believe that

"there needs must be opposition in all things." Learn from your difficulties and disappointments. Be happy for the strength which is being built into your character and personality.

Read the scriptures regularly. Take your seminary work seriously. Help make your Sunday School and Mutual classes strong and worthwhile. Be sure to read the Youth Sections in the Era thoroughly and regularly. Feel free to go to the Lord with your troubles. Don't forget to thank him for your blessings. Count them regularly. Confide in your parents and your bishop when you feel troubled.

7. *Develop a Good Personality.* By a good personality we do not mean a thin veneer of glamor. We mean a personality which stimulates others to be happy, confident, and to feel well-adjusted when they are in your presence. Learn how to stimulate good conversation by asking questions and then being a good listener. This keeps you from constantly harping on your troubles or achievements (especially your imagined ones), your point of view, or your plans. Try to feel relaxed, and be relaxed around others. You will be, if you don't worry too much about yourself, and if you show a good measure of concern about others.

In terms of your life this means that if you will do all you can to make yourself a young lady who can be a true friend, wife, and mother, you will sometime, somewhere, receive fulfillment of all your righteous desires and will have a home, family, and husband of your own.

8. *Plan Properly for the Future.* Modern life demands a great deal of service, training, and education of a young man. By the time he fills a mission, meets his military obligations, and acquires his schooling, marriage will

have been in the background for at least a few years. Young women should realize this is going to happen and should plan to use this waiting period to gain training and education for themselves. It would be wise to plan to attend the schools where these young men will obtain their final education and training. That is one of the reasons the Church has such schools as the Brigham Young University, Ricks College, and other colleges now in the planning stage. In addition the Church has provided Institutes of Religion, Deseret Clubs, and sororities and fraternities through the Lambda Delta Sigma at many, many schools which are not Church-sponsored. All young LDS people should join these organizations and social institutions where they can meet and associate with those of their own faith and belief.

There are other facets to this problem, but the foregoing items should be sufficient to help you find ways of meeting your particular problems as they arise.

CHAPTER TWENTY-ONE

WHEN SHOULD YOUNG PEOPLE START TO GO STEADY?

On January 3, 1960, while speaking to the youth of the Church, President David O. McKay made the following statement.

> Here young people, let me sound a note of warning against going steady too young . . . going steady too early in life is fraught with handicaps to which hopeful, fiery youth should not be subjected.
>
> In the first place, young people are very susceptible — quick to fall in love, and being immature in judgment, may not distinguish between fascination or passion and true admiration or genuine love. (Church News. January 9, 1960, p. 3.)

Young Latter-day Saints who recognize the President of the Church as the prophet, seer, and revelator of God on this earth will not quibble with this advice. They will accept it and make plans for putting it into effect. In order that you will be fully equipped to carry out your decision to do so, think this counsel through fully and carefully. Let us consider both sides of this problem.

"Going steady" is an arrangement in which a boy and a girl have a definite, mutually understood commitment to each other to limit their dates and social activities to each other's company. It is usually understood that there is a definite emotional attachment, and that if either one were to date someone else it would be disturbing and upsetting to the other, even for only one date.

Why Do Young People Go Steady?

1. There is a strong feeling of security. This is true especially for the girl who is assured an escort to dances, parties, and the other social affairs which are so important to young people. The boy may also like the feeling of knowing he will have a companion whenever he desires and so can dismiss from his mind the matter of getting a date.

2. It removes strain of getting acquainted with new personalities. The tension which may make it difficult to adjust to different types of individuals for various dates is absent.

3. Since each new date may have a different set of friends, it is not necessary to get acquainted with them and learn to respond favorably to strangers so often if one has a "steady."

4. One does not always have to be on one's best behavior. A "steady" is like an old shoe which gives a feeling of comfort. "Steadies" have adopted themselves to each other and feel comfortable in each other's presence. They are "in" so to speak and so do not have to be on their best behavior to make a good impression on each other.

5. It is sometimes the custom in a particular community. Anyone who is "anyone" has a "steady." Not to have a "steady" would indicate the boy or girl did not "rate" and was failing socially.

6. Parents sometimes encourage their children to go steady, so they will make good "social adjustments" and be invited to all the dances and parties which parents feel are important for their children to attend. This is especially true of mothers who were not too popular in their own school days and fear the same may be true for their daughters.

7. Some school officials and some Church organizations encourage going steady to insure the success of the
social functions they are promoting.

8. Some young people do not find normal affections
at home, so they seek it as early as possible with a "steady"
who can give them a feeling of "belonging" to someone and
having someone "belong" to them.

9. There seems to be a natural compatibility between
a certain boy and girl.

What Are Some of the Drawbacks of Going "Steady"?

1. The strong emphasis on the reduction of tensions
and of the need for continual adjustment if one has a
"steady" is most disturbing. Sometimes it indicates weak-
ness of personality and satisfaction with an arrest of growth
in character at an age when such preparation is most vital
for adulthood. "Going steady" is no doubt turning social
life into a pleasant "rut" in which one can travel with a
minimum of effort. But it is important to remember that
ruts are found only on backwoods roads. These are generally unimproved or poorly built; they are only seldom
repaired, and all too often lead to unimportant destinations
or "dead ends." It has been said that a rut is a grave with
both ends knocked out. The question which now confronts
those of you who want to go steady too early is whether
you want your lives molded and directed by that kind of
influence? Will the momentary excitement and the need
for putting forth a minimum effort to develop your social
capacity be a blessing or a curse in the future?

2. Naturally going steady frequently leads to a very
strong emotional attachment. Sometimes neither boy nor
girl (although it is generally the boy) desires this turn of

events. The boy may be upset because he wants to go on
a mission, get more education, or he may have a tour of
army duty ahead of him. He may then abruptly break off
the arrangement. At this point there are more considerations than hurt feelings and disappointment to think about.
The boy has not fallen heir to the social handicap the girl
must now overcome. He can ask other girls for dates when
he wants social companionship. The girl, however, is not
so fortunate. She has been out of circulation so long that
other boys never considered her for a dating companion.
They hardly know her, having had little or no opportunity
to get acquainted. They may not even have tried to be
friendly with her because they felt her "steady" would not
approve. Then too, many among them feel that they have
much preparation to make before they are ready for marriage. A girl who has been a "heavy steady" may have
some difficulty overcoming a reputation for being too serious at a time when marriage is not available.

President McKay has emphasized this problem too.

> Ever be mindful that following childhood, youth
> has other obligations besides choosing a mate or hav-
> ing a good time. He must determine first of all what
> kind of character he will develop. He must decide
> what his trade or profession will be, and if he chooses
> a wife, how he will support her and the children.

> Going steady may so enchant the couple that
> these other associated obligations may be given too
> little consideration. (*Church News*. Jan. 9, 1960, p. 3.)

3. "Going steady" too early often leads to intense
emotional feelings which few human beings, let alone young
people, can experience without disaster. President McKay
has made pointed reference to this.

But the worst of early choosing to go steady is that it gives to the young man a sense of familiarity or ownership, and to the young girl, a feeling of belonging, a rapturous state to be consumated rightly by marriage vows. But when experienced by unbridled daring youth, becomes like fruit plucked before it is ripe, something unsavory ... (*Church News*, Jan. 9, 1960, p. 12.)

All too often this continuous familiarity and close association lead the boy and girl to make a serious mistake for which they will have to pay with a lifetime of repentance and regret. Even though they marry each other they may find this does not remedy the situation. Often it makes it worse. Marriage instead of being life's highlight becomes an agonizing duty with all its sweetness turned to bitterness.

4. "Going steady" too early, and thus running the risk of making a poor marriage, is like walking into an automobile agency and buying the first car you see simply because it looks shiny and new. It may be just the car you will buy later on, but you will want to look others over first. You will want to consider engines, upholstery materials, models, styles, and optional equipment as well as price. It is just as wise to consider different personalities in people. Dating gives you a chance to become acquainted with various types of personalities. After you have done this, you are in a position to choose one who will play the complementary role in your life according to your need. "Going steady" too early cripples and limits this power of choice drastically.

5. "Going steady" too early limits one's ability to make and keep friends. Without friends life loses much of its meaning and zest. "Going steady" may mean your circle of friends in high school will be pitifully small. This refers to both boy and girl friends. To rotate dates in high

school will have a lasting effect for good as you develop towards maturity. Each new date will add something to your personal growth and leave you more sure of yourself in your human relationships throughout life.

6. Almost always, a careful analysis of the "love" behind "going steady" shows it has a false glow. It highlights excitement and physical attributes such as beauty of form, ownership of cars, athletic skill, and social acceptance by others.

> As boys and girls finish high school and go to work or to college, their needs change. More sure of their personal value, they gradually cease to ascribe marvelous properties to mere physical attributes, and begin to respond to deep-lying traits of character. This is the kind of love that produces marriage. (*Today's Living*. Morton M. Hunt. Oct. 11, 1959, Harper & Bros., N.Y.)

What Then Is a Suitable Age for "Going Steady"?

Elder Mark E. Petersen answers the above query with a technique Jesus often used.

> When should young people begin going steady? Should it be while they are in junior and senior high school? Or should steady dating be reserved for the time when young people are actually considering marriage, and are old enough to consider it sensibly and realistically, and are capable of carrying on the responsibilities of marriage?" (*Improvement Era*. Mark E. Petersen. Dec. 1959. p. 932.)

On this basis junior high would be much too early. Even at the close of one's senior high school days there would be a very few who could profitably consider going steady. The teens are the dating years, beyond them lies the "going steady" or the courting period.

Part Five

What is Courting?
What Are the Purposes of
Engagement?

CHAPTER TWENTY-TWO

WHAT IS COURTSHIP AND WHAT IS ITS PURPOSE?

Beginning with this topic we are moving out of the present range of your activities into experiences which should normally lie in the future. We shall be looking forward to that time when you are fully ready to "go steady." From here on we shall dignify "going steady" by giving it a name which has more meaning. We shall call it courting. We shall also discuss a type of courting of which the world knows nothing. Here again we shall give it still another name.

Courting has a different purpose from dating. It has no place in the lives of young people until they are able to consider marriage seriously. It is not as firm as an engagement, but it is certainly not as informal as dating. It looks toward a final choice, toward engagement. It has some definite goals among which the following are a few examples.

1. *To explore.* Courting is for the purpose of exploring seriously the type and quality of personality, ideals, and religious faith of a person who might be a suitable partner in the eternal bond of celestial marriage. Courting helps one determine if there is fertile soil for the mature love of marriage. It is well known that unless a husband and wife can work together, worship together, seek mutual recreation, and through their common interests rear a family together, their marriage may be overloaded with risks. Courting should give a preliminary indication of whether two people should plan for celestial marriage.

2. *To gain further maturity.* Dating is more or less a social activity. It lacks the serious purpose and depth of courting. In courting, young people formulate more firmly their outlook on life. They learn how people of the opposite sex think deep in their hearts. Thus they can begin the process of orienting themselves to the hopes and ideals of their future wife or husband.

3. *To prepare for a formal engagement.* Many marriage counselors believe that a somewhat extended courting period is more desirable than a long engagement. While courting involves a firmer and more definite relationship than dating, it is not as rigid and final as the engagement. It is much easier to break off a courtship than an engagement.

Actually the matter of a final choice may be considered more a part of courting than engagement; for example, if after a period of courtship the young man and woman find they are not ready for marriage or that they do not seem well-matched, they can quietly and privately break off their courting and return to other dating arrangements without a great deal of explaining, embarrassment, hurt feelings, and emotional upheaval on their part or the part of their families. The engagement should be a period when young people are not making a choice but are actually preparing for their forthcoming marriage.

Should LDS Men and Women Have a Different Courtship from the People of the World?

You are no doubt thoroughly aware of the fact that the goals of the members of the Church for marriage are different from those of nonmembers. Is it not logical then to assume that people preparing for a temple marriage would require a different type of courtship? If you were traveling directly to New York, you would have to take a different road from that which you would take if you were going to the moon, would you not? Would it not also be necessary to have different clothes, mode of travel, and to make other preparations of a specialized nature?

People of the world enter into a marriage contract which ends with death. Latter-day Saint marriage contracts become firmer and more binding and permanent as time passes. They last for eternity. In line with this unique situation let us consider a plan for a different type of courtship—shall we call it a "temple courtship?"

Why Is a "Temple Courtship" Necessary?

In addition to all the goals of a courtship as carried on by the people of the world, Latter-day Saint boys and girls need to determine the presence of the following additional qualifications in their prospective mates.

1. The presence of a testimony of the truthfulness of the gospel. Without a testimony it is most difficult, if not impossible, to live up fully to the promises made to the Lord when taking one's endowments in the temple. "Going through the temple" by itself will not achieve exaltation for anyone. "Faith without works is dead," we are told by James. Ministers, educators, and others have studied the Church, its program, and achievements. Sometimes parts of its program have been tried out by them in their organizations. But success does not follow these adaptions. It is not the plan alone, *but the testimony of the divine nature of the plan,* which makes it possible for Church members to carry it out. If you are to have an effective temple mar-

riage, you and your partner must have a testimony of the gospel. Whether you do or not can be established during a "temple courtship."

2. Greater emotional maturity. As indicated previously, emotional maturity is characterized by three conditions (1) a young man or a young woman can stand pain and suffering with courage and faith when it is necessary to do so; (2) he or she can pursue goals in life which make it necessary to wait for rewards; (3) he or she takes a deep interest in others and is concerned about their welfare and happiness.

Members of the Church need a stronger, more complete development of these attributes. They are working for a celestial exaltation which will demand faith and courage. Rewards for paying tithes and rendering service must wait, sometimes until the next life. Unless the young couple have a deep interest in others, they will find little joy in doing temple work, in officering the auxiliaries, in going on missions, in serving in bishoprics and stake presidencies, or even as General Authorities. The wives of these men who preside over wards, stakes, and in the Church generally must have unusual strength of character and emotional maturity. Where better, than during courtship with temple marriage in mind, can it be established that one's prospective mate has this maturity?

3. Strong and deeply ingrained habits and character. Life is always a struggle, especially if you are striving for a championship. All who aspire to a championship must be strong from righteous living, training, and thinking. These are things which should not merely be wished for. They should be lived and worked for. You must have an

opportunity to look deeply into the soul of a man or woman to know whether these habits and character traits are there. A "temple courtship" will give you that insight.

How Is a "Temple Courtship" Different from an Ordinary Courtship?

There are several very distinct differences.

1. A temple courtship is not based on a desire for excitement or physical sensation. Whereas an ordinary courtship may merely be an unplanned continuation of a series of dates which have been "fun," a temple courtship is an activity carried on to reach a goal, an ideal—the finding of a suitable partner for a partnership with God.

2. There is a strong and definite attitude of respect for others and self. In a "temple courtship" the welfare of the other person is paramount. There is a desire to be kindly, to help, to build up, and to assist one's dating partner in every way. This is done so there can be trust and confidence and a revelation of one's innermost ideals and loyalties to a person who would otherwise be a stranger. The establishing of this feeling of rapport to a degree not possible in an ordinary courtship is most vital.

3. The "temple courtship" proceeds at a more leisurely pace. There is no quick development of emotion which leads to a marriage in a matter of hours, days, or a few weeks. The young couple are aware that it will take time to achieve all that needs to be done before a sound decision can be reached concerning marriage.

4. There is a deliberate attempt to participate in a wider variety of activities and to become acquainted with

a greater circle of friends and relatives. These activities would certainly include regular attendance at church services. In addition the couple will very likely participate together in promoting the program of the Church by serving as dance instructors in MIA, as speech and drama leaders in the ward or stake, as M-Men and Gleaner leaders, or as participants in the June conference festivals in singing, music, or drama. They might spend some of their time helping each other to achieve Master M-Men or Golden Gleaner awards. Since World War II it has been necessary for many of our young men to render military service. This along with going on a mission and completing lengthy educational requirements has made it necessary for the young men to postpone marriage for a few years. In such instances some young people may spend some time doing temple work together for the dead. At some of our Church schools courting couples find temple excursions are an unequaled highlight of their association.

5. During "temple courtship" there is also more contact with each other's friends, relatives, and parents. It is difficult to learn more about people's characters, personalities, and interests, than can be ascertained by associating in their homes and closed-circle entertainments. One man said, in fun mostly but with some justification, that if a boy wants to know how a girl will treat him as a husband he should observe how she treats her brother. Since all people, in a sense, marry each other's families, young couples should become acquainted with their prospective in-laws during courtship. Dating may bring little or no contact with these situations. In a "temple courtship" they should be highlighted as much as possible. They should associate in

each other's homes not only on social occasions but also during times when normal, routine activities are going on.

6. There should be ample and constant opportunity for repeated, sincere, and serious discussion of life as the young couple will know it after marriage, throughout life, and in the eternities. This could lead to a desire to discuss these problems with parents, the bishop, or some other Church leader. Temple courtship leads away from the light-minded, frivolous interests and activities of the teen-age to a maturing of outlook in preparation for adult living.

If the special purpose and activities of a "temple court-ship" are carried out, a young couple can feel much more secure in its hope for a happy and successful temple marriage and can more confidently enter into the engagement period.

CHAPTER TWENTY-THREE

WHAT ARE THE PURPOSES OF THE ENGAGEMENT?

To become engaged is to make semi-final one's choice of a marriage partner. The engagement ring is the symbol of this decision although the ring is not absolutely necessary. During depressions, and for other acceptable reasons, the young couple may not have the means for an expensive ring and may have to settle for a dignified wedding band later on. Generally there is an announcement, a declaration to the world at large, that the couple intends to wed. It is in effect an acknowledgment that the couple is asking for a place in society and that it is entering upon life seriously and with full intent to make an adult contribution to the community.

What Should an Engagement Achieve?

It is to be hoped that making the final choice will be more a part of courting than the engagement. Engagement is a time of emotional and spiritual union. There is a more firm welding together of ideals, aims, and goals. The couple draw close together in feelings, hopes, and beliefs. They complete their plans for the time and place of marriage, place and kind of residence, and employment. Items which in the past were of individual interest, must now be considered from a mutual point of view.

How Long Should the Engagement Last?

Extensive studies indicate that the length of the engagement is a very important factor in a happy marriage.

Its length is a matter of great interest to young people. It would be reassuring if a definite period of time for a satisfactory engagement could be indicated, but this does not seem possible. However, it can be said that it should be long enough so that its purposes desired can be realized. This will depend on the length and nature of the courtship. Most marriage counselors feel the engagement should be not less than six months. An important study of a large group of people who were happily married revealed the startling fact that their average engagement was five years in length! This is not necessarily a basic standard for length of engagements, but it does indicate that time is important. There is a type of growth and development which does not begin until the young couple is definitely committed to each other by the engagement. The engagement period should be one of supreme happiness. It is doubtful that any period in a person's life except marriage could hold possibilities for greater joy. This is especially true if attention is focused on spiritual and emotional preparation. Such an emphasis creates a glow which lasts throughout eternity. But it should be remembered that the values from engagements cannot be hastened into ripeness. Wise young people will not cheat themselves by by-passing a reasonably adequate engagement period.

What Special Problems Does Engagement Create?

When young people are thrown together as much and as intimately as they are during engagement, they may come to feel an attraction for each other which is difficult to control. This condition is so commonplace that some people feel that an engaged couple can take liberties with each other than should be reserved only for those who are married. But the Lord has not given engaged couples the rights he has given those who are married. The marriage vow still separates chastity from unchastity. Physical attraction receives its *permanent* powers for joy through being subject to the spiritual goals of life. To use it in any other way, at any other time can only have an unhappy result. The law of chastity applies at all times, and while the period of engagement may be more intimate and more like marriage in some respects than courting, it is still not marriage. It lacks many important and vital elements which pertain only to those who are legally and lawfully married. Only after marriage are the couple able and ready to welcome children, and this accomplishment, not sense satisfaction, is the basic reason God created men and women.

By way of illustration we might compare the full use of the powers of procreation to the use of electricity in a newly built home. As long as the house is properly wired when the electricity is brought in, everything works to the advantage of the builder. However, if the electricity is introduced before the wiring is complete, the result will be burned-out wiring, blown fuses, a possible fire which might destroy the house or even electrocution of some member of the family.

Used before complying with all the legal and lawful requirements of marriage, the mating urge is likewise destructive. Its power must be utilized only within the marriage bond. There it has been designed by our Heavenly Father to serve several purposes and bring joy and progress into human life. Outside of that relationship, even if it is misused but once, it is highly destructive. Such use results in a painful and long-lasting spiritual shock or even death instead of a flow of life, joy, and power forever.

This temptation to be physically intimate will be greatly reduced if young people will observe certain precautions such as the following:

1. Pray together from time to time at the beginning of their dates or at times when they feel especially tempted.

2. Make a promise never to do anything of which they would not like to have their parents and their Heavenly Father informed.

3. Reduce the number of times and the duration of their activities together, especially if they face a long engagement.

4. Always have plenty of activity available to keep their minds off each other as persons.

5. Spend less time alone. They should spend much of their time in each other's homes and with their respective families in order that their minds and activities can be centered on their own future home and children and not on their personal emotions.

When Should an Engagement Be Broken?

A satisfactory answer to this problem depends entirely on what is at the basis of the disharmony. Most engaged couples will discover small faults in each other which even the radiance of love cannot hide. Minor items of carelessness in personal habits, dress, speech, etc., may begin to irritate. If the couple can make a satisfactory adjustment in these minor matters, they will find that such willingness to please each other will add strength to their engagement.

However, if the basis of the trouble lies deep in the emotional make-up of one or the other, and becomes more irritating all the time, the young couple should pause and reflect on its eventual effect on their marriage. Before breaking the engagement they should seek qualified counsel and talk the matter over thoroughly. It may be they are demanding one another to fill impossible roles. It takes time and the proper conditions for these personality needs to become manifest and make themselves felt. They sometimes become evident only after an engagement has lasted a reasonable length of time.

If prayerful consideration and wise counsel indicate there are insurmountable obstacles to a happy marriage, the engagement should be broken quickly, quietly, and in as kindly a way as possible. Each should try to reduce the hurt for the other. There should be no blaming, gossip, or name calling. It is distressing to break an engagement, of that there can be no doubt. A ring may have been bought, congratulations and best wishes received. Plans have been laid for the wedding, a home, and children. Pleasant memories of interesting and thrilling dates are remembered when the couple think of each other. Now having to discard all this, together with having to make explanations to one's friends and relatives together with having to endure the gossip which is sure to ensue makes breaking an engagement very uninviting.

But one must remember that the problems of breaking an engagement are mild compared to those of obtaining a divorce. Court proceedings necessary to divorce cut deeply. If there are children, their custody must be determined. They love both parents and can't understand why the parents do not love each other. Sometimes the children feel neither parent loves them or they wouldn't be breaking up the home. If there is a remarriage, the children acquire a third parent—to some children an emotionally upsetting situation. In addition there can be the problems which come with half-brothers and half-sisters. Then too, a child in the home by a former marriage is a constant reminder of the failure of the previous union. Property settlements must often be made which result in bitter and long-drawn out contention. The husband and wife have formed a much stronger attachment in marriage than they had during courtship. The strife and disagreement of divorce are often soul-destroying. To tear out the roots of a former love leaves scars which psychologists say are permanent. Innocent or guilty, as far as the cause of the divorce is concerned, the emotional hurt is devastating to all parties.

Again the woman bears the greater burden. Many women who are divorcees find that the respect with which they were treated before marriage has vanished; and this through no fault of their own. They are spoken of as "grass widows" and are sometimes rudely treated and regarded by base men who think they are easy targets for immoral advances. Divorced women may suffer from lonesomeness. They often lack escorts to social events. Divorce may partially destroy one's confidence in the ability to enter successfully into another marriage. Breaking an engagement is like having a small cloud pass over one's life. In comparison, a divorce is a gray pall which never disappears entirely.

Young people should be as sure as possible they are prepared to make a prudent choice before they are engaged.

Though their aim should be to make as perfect a match as possible, they must be realistic in what they expect of each other. No one is entirely perfect. But it is important for them to seek as firm a foundation as possible for marriage, and not build their future on quicksand.

CHAPTER TWENTY-FOUR

HOW CAN YOU BE REASONABLY SURE
YOU HAVE MADE A WISE CHOICE?

It most certainly is not difficult to get into a state of excitement which people call love. What worries thoughtful young people is whether this is truly love, and *will they stay in love?* There is little doubt about their feelings at the time of their marriage. The source of doubt is rather whether the couple will find enough in each other's ideals, personalities, and characters to remain attracted to each other when the physical phase of their interest takes a place of secondary importance as it inevitably will.

In order that you might have some assistance in making a pre-engagement measurement of your adaptability for marriage with a certain person there follows a scale which you can use over and over again until you have made a final decision.

How Shall We Evaluate This Scale?

This scale should be used when you become seriously interested in someone and have had a courting relationship with them. After you have been engaged and are about ready to marry, it would be well to use the scale again. This time the last two questions would also be included.

You should be forewarned against the "halo" effect in using a rating scale such as this. The "halo" effect is the tendency to (1) to mark a scale as you *wish* and *want* a situation to be and (2) the tendency to let one trait in

which a person rates very high affect you in your ratings
on other traits. For this reason it might be desirable to let
your parents use the rating scale and then compare the results with your own rating. You will be able to have much
more confidence in your ratings if you can compare them
with those of someone who is more objective. If you do
not feel you want to present it to your parents, you might
have a trusted friend mark the scale.

		Yes	Partly	No
1.	We are members of the same Church.	10	5	0
2.	We have the same degree of interest in the Church and its program.	8	4	0
3.	We have both been active in the Church all our lives.	6	3	0
4.	I have the feeling my proposed mate will help me develop my personality.	5	3	0
5.	We have the same ideals con-cerning the purpose of marriage as a partnership with God.	5	3	0
6.	We have the approval of our parents for marriage.	8	4	0
7.	We both feel God is pleased with our choice of each other.	8	4	0
8.	We have approximately the same economic background.	4	2	0
9.	We are both mature and old enough to settle down.	10	5	0

		Yes	Partly	No
10.	Neither one of us is trying to get away from a home or environment we dislike.	10	5	0
11.	We both have good health, (Based on a doctor's examination)	5	3	0
12.	I am prepared to meet competition and make a living. (Boy)	8	4	0
13.	I can properly, economically, and wisely conduct a household. (Girl)	5	3	0
14.	We are both honest in our dealings with each other and others.	8	4	0
15.	We are morally clean or have made restitution with our bishop if we have transgressed.	10	5	0
16.	We both have clean personal habits of dress and grooming.	5	3	0
17.	We can discuss personal problems with each other without getting angry.	5	3	0
18.	We are willing to accept each other with the idea we both have imperfections and will likely continue to have them.	5	3	0
19.	We have had a "temple courtship."	10	5	0
20.	We consistently bring out joyful and harmonious behavior when we are around each other.	8	4	0

	Yes	Partly	No
21. We have determined that it would be practical to combine our heredities.	5	3	0
22. We could both get a recommend without having to break bad habits.	8	4	0
23. We are thoroughly acquainted with each other's ideal and attitudes.	5	3	0
24. We have full trust and confidence in each other.	5	3	0
25. We have both dated enough other persons so we can compare our proposed mate with other people.	5	3	0
26. Our recreational interests are compatible and not conflicting.	5	3	0
27. We have about the same educational interests and background.	5	3	0
28. We enjoy talking with each other about a variety of topics.	5	3	0
29. We have had feelings of respect toward each other during courtship.	8	4	0
30. We are proud to present each other to the best people we know.	5	3	0
31. Our personalities are enough alike so we can work as a team.	5	3	0

	Yes	Partly	No
32. We are about equally ener-getic in our approach to life and its activities.	5	3	0
33. We have both had the ideal of a temple marriage for some time.	8	4	0
34. Our engagement has been sufficiently long to prepare us emotionally and spiritually for marriage.	5	3	0
35. Our engagement has been free of serious, highly emo-tional, and prolonged quarrels.	8	4	0

A perfect score would be 217. This of course is an impossible score because human beings are not perfect. A score of around 200 would be excellent, 195 very good, 185 good, and 175 fair.

A perfect score for an *engaged* person would be 230. A score of around 213 would be excellent, 208 very good, 198 good, and 188 fair.

These scores are certainly not absolute, but they will give you something definite on which to base your decision. Differences of ten or twenty points may or may not be significant. In fact, a person could score very high in all items but one, and a zero score on that point would indicate that a marriage might run into serious difficulty. Scales such as these only help to bring a problem more sharply into focus; they do not and cannot provide a ready-made answer.

Part Six

Temple Marriage
Versus
Civil Marriage

CHAPTER TWENTY-FIVE

WHY IS A TEMPLE MARRIAGE THE ONLY KIND FOR YOU?

President Brigham Young said that if young people could look into the eternities and see the full value of a temple marriage they would crawl across the continent on their hands and knees to obtain it. Since he was a prophet and knew whereof he spoke, we can accept this as a true statement.

The Apostle Paul twice bore a like witness. When recounting his vision of paradise he testifies of hearing "unspeakable words which it is not lawful for a man to utter." (2 Corinthians 12:4.) Again he wrote, "Eye hath not seen nor ear heard, neither has it entered into the heart of man the things which God hath prepared for them that love him." (1 Corinthians 2:9.)

Evidently the blessings of a celestial exaltation are beyond human understanding. No doubt a great part of the sorrow sinners experience after death comes from a realization of what they have lost by pursuing earthly pleasures. Some of the Saints seem to have had an inkling of what God has prepared. They felt it was worth giving up earthly pleasure, the goodwill of neighbors, their places in their own families, earthly wealth and fame, and in not a few instances, life itself.

The problem now is to help you catch this vision so that you will make a firm, irrevocable decision to take nothing less than a temple marriage. The decision will have to be yours. It must involve all of you — all your actions, planning, and decisions in every field of living. Let us examine the case for and against a "time" marriage as compared to an eternal, celestial marriage. First, what are the drawbacks to a "time" marriage?

1. It is in a pattern foreign to the one God gave his children. In the beginning Father Adam and Mother Eve were married for eternity. God said man was not to put asunder what he had joined. Scripture also points out most definitely "that man is not without woman in the Lord." A "time" marriage is a false start. It is devoid of confidence in God's plan. Sometimes it is a vote of no confidence in themselves or each other when the young couple decides on a "time" marriage to see whether "it will work"—with the provision they can be sealed in the temple later on. How successful would any difficult venture be if people approached it with that attitude? How can it help lowering the chance for a mature love to develop between the bride and groom if they assume an attitude of doubt and lack of faith toward the most important step they will take in life?

2. The children are not born under the covenant. They are not automatically members of the eternal family unit. Have you ever thought of the wonderful blessings you have as an American-born citizen? How much greater a blessing it is to be born under the covenant! A "time" marriage will deny your children that great blessing.

3. Those who marry out of the temple can never truly have a temple marriage. They can only be sealed. To have one's courtship and engagement reach its climax in a temple marriage is a privilege which comes only once.

A temple sealing can be most wonderful and is as filled with joy as a temple marriage to those who could not have its services at the time of their marriage, but those who choose a "time" marriage in preference to a temple marriage have passed up a measure of joy they will never again be privileged to experience.

4. A man and woman who marry out of the temple will not have a full measure of the strength of the gospel working for them in their lives. What might the result be? No eternal family. No celestial exaltation. In extreme cases, one may follow a downward path so far that he is denied a part in the first resurrection. That is like getting a jail sentence of a thousand years. What a dreary, dreadful prospect!

5. Separation at death leaves men and women looking toward a lonesome condition where they will live "separately and singly" throughout all eternity. A long time indeed to yearn for the soul-satisfying companionship, friendship, and feelings of love experienced by righteous men and women in the family relationship!

6. Many young people who have settled for less than a temple marriage have lived to regret it deeply. They have grown so far away from the Church that when the time came for their children to be married in the temple they have not been permitted to enter and share in the joyous occasion. They have been separated—left outside. In a sense this is a preview of things to come. In eternity, those who are not sealed by the power of the priesthood lose the children they have gained on earth. They will also forfeit the ability to have an increase of the life-giving powers and relationships. They will not have the power

Gateway or Barrier?

of increase—no "eternal lives." There will be no prospect of entering into a loving relationship with spirit children or of creating worlds upon which to place them to help them attain their exaltation.

7. Those who have not entered into an eternal marriage will be ministering angels to those who have. They will have to help others go on to greater glory and joy. The full fruits of their labors will not be theirs. For all eternity they will have to give them up, pass them on to someone else who was strong enough, wise enough, faithful enough, to secure these blessings to themselves and their children. When one thinks of how unsatisfying it must be to minister eternally to others and not be working for one's own blessing and exaltation, it should strengthen one greatly in the determination never to settle for less than a temple marriage.

8. Those who have complied with the laws of the gospel have been told by God in section 76:58-59 in the Doctrine and Covenants:

> Wherefore, as it is written, they are gods, even the sons of God—wherefore, all things are theirs, whether life or death, or things present, or things to come, all are theirs, and they are Christ's, and Christ is God's.

Would you feel bad if you foolishly failed to comply with the terms of an agreement with an earthly person and lost an inheritance of $100,000,000—especially if it had been in your power to do so and you had lost it because you had been shortsighted, material minded, and impatient. How empty the souls of men must be when they comprehend how great their loss has been if they lose eternal life. It is beyond human imagination to estimate the loss of these blessings.

9. Those in the telestial kingdom will never see the Father and the Son. Those in the terrestrial kingdom will never see Elohim or God the Father. Men who have stood in the presence of Jesus Christ bear testimony that they would give all their earthly possessions for the privilege of standing in his presence again for a few minutes. Can anyone estimate what it would mean to dwell there eternally, or how great the sorrow will be if this unspeakable blessing were lost forever?

Now let us look at the other side of the coin so to speak, and see the advantages of a true temple marriage.

1. You are in harmony with the Lord's way. This brings peace of mind, a feeling of security, of acceptance by him of your way of life.

2. A temple marriage is in harmony with the sacred nature of marriage. Marriage is an event in life which exemplifies the truth of the Savior's declaration: "Man shall not live by bread alone." Men and women have a deep longing for a fulfillment of the great spiritual powers connected with being husband and wife, father and mother. If ever the human soul thirsts for "living water," it is at this time. When a couple comes to the temple truly prepared for a partnership with God, they experience a great spiritual sense of fulfillment. At no other time and in no other place do human beings have the privilege of sensing the joy and strength of womanhood and manhood as they do when they kneel at the altar in the house of the Lord and accept their responsibilities as co-creators with God.

3. Statistics indicate that temple marriage greatly increases the chances for marital happiness. Conversely, it decreases the chance for failure.

4. It provides, if the commandments are kept, the means of keeping your family together in the eternities.

5. Young men and women who are determined to be married in the temple are strengthened against entrapment by Satan. They are better able to "stay on course." They are not nearly so likely to be lured into a teen marriage or lose their virtue.

6. A temple marriage opens the door to eternal progression. How much satisfaction and joy that implies no one can begin to fathom.

7. It puts at the service of the family the powers of the priesthood for inspiration, guidance, healing of the sick, etc.

8. It makes it possible for men and women to become as God is.

9. A goal of temple marriage rules out elopements and secret marriages. The young couple are assured the aid and assistance of parents and Church leaders in making a wise and suitable choice in marriage. It largely eliminates from consideration those who would not be suitable.

10. All who marry in the temple must achieve above average strength of character. This training is invaluable as an aid to success in business and social life.

11. It does away with the temptation to enter a "part-member" marriage. If you will think on the section on "part-member" marriages, you will realize what a blessing this is.

12. If there is any event in life which should be sur-rounded with beauty it is your marriage. There could never be a lovelier place and more sympathetic, co-opera-tive, and spiritually trained people to do this than in the temple. The world with its turmoil, sin, and lack of sen-sitivity for eternal values has been shut out. In the holy, dedicated atmosphere of the temple all thoughts are turned to the lasting values of life by the instructions in the bride's and bridegroom's rooms. These are reinforced powerfully by the endowment. Then comes marriage in a room espe-cially set apart for that purpose. One almost feels that it is hallowed by the thousands of eternal marriages which have begun there. No words can adequately describe the beauty of a temple marriage. Nor can it be estimated how much it contributes to the welfare, success and happiness of those who are united there. Many persons declare that the beauty of the temple ceremony is something they have never before experienced.

This then is the comparison. The choice is yours— yours to make *now!*

CHAPTER TWENTY-SIX

WHAT PREPARATIONS ARE NECESSARY
FOR A TEMPLE MARRIAGE?

It is not uncommon to find that young people in the Church are not specifically informed on the requirements for a temple marriage. This is tragic because some of this preparation takes years if it is to be effective. A genuine temple marriage will be sealed by the Holy Spirit of Promise. It is not the result of a few weeks or months of hasty, shallow repentance. The value of "cleaning up" for a few weeks, of attending priesthood and Sacrament meetings a short time, of making a contribution, which some would like to call tithing, and then asking for a temple recommend is hardly worth considering. Far too many such members make promises to the Lord which they simply are not able to keep later on no matter how good their intentions were at the time. God has said he will not be mocked. If we are unfaithful in our vows, he has no choice but to turn us over to the buffetings of Satan where the chances of overcoming our weaknesses may be much less than we now realize.

In order that you might be prepared for the blessings of this great event let us list the requirements for a temple marriage.

I. *A Temple Recommend.* This privilege to use the Lord's house is granted by the ward bishop. He will ask a series of questions, most of which are given him by the First Presidency, in order to determine your worthiness. After he has filled out the form and signed it, you must go to the stake president and go through the same procedure with him. Be sure you arrange for your recommend before you announce your plans for marriage. This could save you much embarrassment and possible sorrow.

II. *General Gospel Requirements.* These could be described as elements of faithful membership in the Church. You should be:

1. A strict keeper of the Word of Wisdom as set forth in the 89th section of the Doctrine and Covenants.
2. Consistent and regular attender of priesthood and Sacrament meetings.
3. A willing participant in the program of the Church.
4. An honest payer of tithes, offerings, and donations.
5. Honest and upright in dealing with your fellow men.
6. Clean in speech and thought.
7. A firm and willing supporter of the Authorities of the Church.
8. It is matter of *FIRST IMPORTANCE* that you be morally clean. This means that if there has been a moral transgression that the matter has been presented to the bishop or stake president and clearance has been received from them.

III. *Sereological Test and License.* Before a couple can be married in the temple, they must comply with the requirements of the civil law of the state in which the temple is located. Couples who have a civil marriage in a state where such a requirement exists and wish to be sealed must have a blood test before they can be sealed in the temple.

IV. *Have Own Temple Endowments.* Both parties of the prospective marriages must receive their own endowments previous to the ceremony. This is generally done on the day of their marriage, but many young couples may have obtained their endowments before their nuptial day.

V. *Arrange Marriage Date and Time.* When setting the date for their marriage, a young couple should check with the temple to find out which days are set apart for the performance of marriages.

The foregoing steps can be quickly stated, but they may be fulfilled only by consistent and continuous living of the gospel during the years preceding marriage.

Part Seven

Is There Such a Thing as Marriage Insurance?

CHAPTER TWENTY-SEVEN

WHAT CAN YOUNG COUPLES DO TO INSURE A HAPPY MARRIED LIFE?

Up to this point our interest has been preparation for a partnership with a member of the opposite sex and God, our Eternal Father. Our ultimate goal, however, is not preparation, but participation. Actually being married and making that marriage a success. Good preparation is absolutely vital. It is the foundation. But, you will find after your marriage ceremony that you have only arrived at the beginning of the road. Since most of you will not have the opportunity later to discuss the problems encountered in marriage, let us consider them now.

1. Human beings are different from animals. Human beings do not work, play, or express affection instinctively. Every achievement of the human race is a learned reaction. Great music, literature, architecture, and science are the result of learned behavior. These all take knowledge, understanding, and proper perspective. So does marriage. Sometimes the failure to achieve happiness is due to ignorance. People who have an excellent education may be as uninformed on how people should act toward each other as man and wife as a person with limited education. Then again there are people who believe marriage gives them certain privileges regardless of their partner's feelings and desires. Unfortunately under either of these circumstances love and affection dwindle and die. True love is the greatest of all arts. It needs to be understood and practised that

way. Generally those who pretend to know all about these personal problems are the most misinformed. Too much of their information is covered with "gutter dust."

It is most helpful for a couple to talk to parents, a physician with a gospel point of view, a qualified bishop, teacher, or an experienced and trusted counselor about the intimate problems of marriage a few months before the ceremony. Even if no counsel has been sought or received in connection with this problem one point should never be forgotten. It is this: one's actions are never offensive or love destroying if kindness, true affection, and consideration for each other's happiness and welfare are the motivating force. This is most certainly true of the intimate relationship of marriage.

2. Remember that being happily and successfully married is generally not so much a matter of marrying the right person as it is *being the right person*. If there is an axiom in marriage, that is it. Wealth, beauty, social position, and education are wonderful if properly regarded, but they are not necessary for a happy marriage. One of the first thoughts which occurs to young people when they experience adjustment difficulties during the early years of married life is that if they had married someone else they would not have any difficulties. It is true they might not have the particular difficulties they are having, but they most certainly would have other problems in their place. Successful marriage is built on a wise choice of a partner, but its attainment rests on the ability to do one's part fully. to make the necessary contribution to one's mate and children.

3. You should realize that a change in perspective must come into your life after marriage. Whereas you have been privileged to look at life from your own point of view to a large extent, you now must hesitate and also look at it from another's standpoint. Not only are you dealing with an adult who has had different experiences from those you have had, but that person is of the opposite sex, and by training and physiology has different feelings, desires, ideas, and goals in life. He or she will approach problems from a different orientation than you will. You will need to be sympathetic to this difference and make reasonable allowance for it.

4. There is a possibility that the change in interests, perspective, and activities which are associated with marriage will affect personality. The closeness of the marriage relationship may bring out certain tendencies which before were weak and barely noticeable. People are sometimes heard to say that their husbands or wives have undergone a great change since marriage. This is especially true of people who have not matured sufficiently emotionally. When, in marriage, they are called upon to make sacrifices and adjustments, they are unable to do so. Instead they show infantile reactions like sulking spells, violent temper tantrums, and unsatiable demands for manifestations of reassurance, and love. If such is the case, it is well to seek help from a qualified counselor. Most universities have people on their staffs who can be of assistance. Sometimes there are lay people, especially Church leaders, of maturity and experience who can help. This problem is most difficult to meet without experienced, professionally. trained help.

5. Practically all people, even the best-matched couples, will undergo a change in their feelings toward their
spouses. This change is a let-down in the kind and degree
of interest in each other as persons after marriage. There
are several reasons for this condition. The first is that it
is simply impossible to live an adult life and continue to be
as intensely interested in each other personally as people
are during courting and engagement. Such an emotional
tempo is not natural to normal life. Secondly, the halo of
love, having served its purpose, fades somewhat. Now for
the first time one's partner is seen for what he or she is,
a human being. Little faults, failings, and shortcomings
which existed but which could not be seen through the rose-
tinted haze of courtship are now outlined sharply by the
sober light of reality. It has been well said that young people should keep their eyes wide open before marriage and
half shut afterwards. Unfortunately they do just the opposite. If young people would be aware of these changes,
their adjustment in marriage would be easier and achieved
more quickly.

6. At times people tend to remain as secluded emotionally and socially after marriage as they were during
courtship and engagement. Too much of anything, no
matter how good it is, soon becomes distasteful and even
nauseating. Couples who do not keep in contact with
friends and neighbors and who are constantly together
may sour on each other. This is often true of professional
people. A famous movie and TV couple have just an-
nounced the break-up of their marriage of twenty years for
this reason. While they were working together, literally
twenty-four hours a day, building their financial empire,

they were wrecking their marriage. People should have enough activity of their own that they do not lose their identities. Marriage is intended to create a healthy, normal ego-status, not to destroy it by total dependency on one's mate.

7. Try to see yourself as others see you. What you discover may not fit into your self-concept, but it will help you be a much better husband or wife.

8. At the beginning of your marriage establish certain patterns of behavior which are acceptable to both of you. If you want your partner to change, offer to wipe out one of your own faults if your mate will do the same. Say to your mate, "Look, if you'll pick up your bath towels, I'll stop squeezing the toothpaste in the middle." Trade faults, that way both can save face. Routines for conducting household affairs should be established. Faithful use of a family council is wonderfully helpful. In fact, it is indispensable in a home if everyone is to achieve the greatest development and happiness.

9. Try to set up certain activities together, which are peculiar to you as a couple and which will result in drawing and keeping you together all during life, especially when your family is grown. This might be a recreational pursuit such as photography, fishing, or traveling. It might be cultural such as participating in a singing or instrumental group. Again it might be a great interest in missionary work or genealogical research. The goal is to work together as a team in something which is relaxing and re-creating. Something which gives joy and zest to counter-balance the deadening effect of routine activities. Try to bring beauty into your lives. This can be done by raising

flowers, improving the home, acquiring a library of lovely, inspiring recordings, or good literature.

10. Be willing to discuss your problems. Keep the communication lines open. When people disagree, they often try to solve their problems by refusing to discuss them. But the problems and their effects remain. In fact they spread and increase until the couple is totally out of effective contact. Don't let the communication lines break down so completely that you need the help of a marriage counselor to reestablish them.

a. Discuss your problems as objectively as you can. Don't try to prove you are right or argue to defend your position. Think only of establishing harmony and understanding. Suspect your own motives more than you do your mates in this attempt to adjust your marriage problems.

b. Tackle a problem as soon as possible after it arises. Fires are most easily put out when they are small. So are arguments. The smallest grudge has a big effect if it is allowed to linger. The advice is most excellent that a husband and wife should never let the sun go down on an unresolved disagreement.

c. Try to see the problem in its total frame of reference and not solely from your own point of view. To illustrate how a point of view can vary according to one's perspective let us consider how differently a microbe and a human being view a mixture of flour and soot. The microbe views this mixture as black and white boulders over which it must crawl. A human being sees it not as separate black and white particles but as a gray mass. If people look at their problems only from their own point of view, they are overwhelmed by their size. From their individual perspective their opinions are always right (white), while those of other people are always wrong (black).

11. Take time to count your blessings frequently. Do so together and with your family when it arrives. Abraham Lincoln said, "Men are about as happy as they make up their minds to be." When you retire, recount to each other the joys and blessings of the day. There is no quicker way to bury your sorrows and take the sting out of defeat than to count your blessings. It will sweeten and purify the soul and keep healthy your love and appreciation for each other.

12. There is a great paradox or apparent contradiction in life. It is: People need love most when they deserve it least. Stop and think about this. Have you not, when you felt insecure, worried, upset, and unhappy been unkind, unco-operative, and downright hostile to those who loved you and wanted to help you in your hour of need? If you will remember your own needs at such times you may be able to help your mate when he or she finds himself or herself in such a situation. Keeping in mind this peculiar twist in human nature will avert harsh words, and deep emotional wounds.

13. Attend to your family prayers with regularity and faithfulness. It has been said that sinning keeps men from praying, and praying keeps men from sinning. Millions will testify that nothing helps so much in the home as family prayer. It is practially impossible to be unkind, selfish,

and disloyal to those who kneel with you daily as you be-seech the Lord in behalf of each other and your children.

One study of family life found that cohesiveness was the most important factor in a family in rearing happy, nor-mal, well-adjusted children. It is truly well said that the family which plays and prays together stays together.

14. Keep your partnership with God strong and ac-tive. In the earlier part of this study the statement was made that a man and woman will love each other in the same measure as they love God. This love of God must have a definite form of expression. The Church through its many organizations provides opportunity for that ex-pression. You have heard of, or possibly experienced, the increase in love and loyalty which come into a family when a son and brother is called on a mission. The same is true in a measure when Father and Mother support each other in Church activities. The real love, devotion, and affec-tion they feel for each other will in a large measure be a direct reflection of their love of God. Marriage as a partner-ship with God is not a figure of speech. It is a necessity for those who want the greatest love and affection in their own homes.

15. Keep life beautiful and in balance by occasionally moving away from earth life toward the eternities in your activities. This can be done by going back to the temple regularly. Temple work is for the purpose of tying our ancestors to us in a great family unit. Again a labor of love is reflected back into the family.

All things earthly tend to fade and lose their lustre as time goes on. But LDS men and women do not need to have this deterioration take place in their lives. They can

go back to the temple regularly and renew the sparkle and
beauty of their own faith and lives. Revisiting the temple
will brighten, renew, and revitalize their own marriage
vows. They will again remember the transcendent beauty
and sweetness of the day on which they pledged themselves to each other. Some people insure everything.
Everything except their marriages. Maybe it is because
no marriage insurance is available. But this insurance is
available to members of the Church who participate in
building the kingdom of God, and who go to the temple
and try constantly to be worthy co-creators with God.
There is direct evidence that these activities are truly
marriage insurance.

Some years ago, as partly recorded in *The Improvement Era* of October 1948, an attempt was made
to determine whether temple marriage is a deterrent to
divorce . . . it was decided to select one year and to
study the conditions of those married in that year. The
year 1936 was chosen. It was far enough away from
the present to expect married people to have settled
down in peace or otherwise. Moreover, those married
in 1936 have passed through the war period when
divorce became popular.

Three temple areas were chosen: Salt Lake, St.
George, and Arizona. The attempt was made to trace
all Latter-day Saint marriages in those areas, in and
out of the temples. The marriages fell into three
classes: 1. married in the temple, 2. married by Church
authorities outside of the temple (by bishops and stake
presidents), and 3. married by civil authority only. The
present status of about thirteen percent of the marriages could not be found; but eighty-seven percent
were found; and their marriage status learned. The
results were approximately the same in all three areas

so the findings must be reliable. Combining the results from all three areas it was found that of those married in the temple, 83.9 percent were active to some extent in the Church, while by those married by Church authorities, but outside of the temple, only 40.6 percent were active in the Church, and 37.6 percent of those married by civil authorities were active in the Church. Temple marriage clearly leads to an orderly faithful life in the Church. It may well be gathered from these figures that those who have the faith and wisdom to marry in the temple are carrying forward the work of the Church.

Among those married in the temple 6.4 percent of the couples had been divorced during the fifteen years of the study. However of those married by Church authorities, outside the temple, there were nearly two and one half times more divorces, namely 15.6 percent. Among those married by civil authorities the number rose to three times that of temple marriages, namely 19.4 percent.

These figures carefully and laboriously assembled declare that temple marriages are a protection against divorce.

If a man and woman are really in love and want that love to endure, they should fit themselves for marriage in the temple. The temple endowment and the sealing for eternal companionship become powerful means of achieving joy on earth and in the heavens beyond. (*Improvement Era*. John A. Widtsoe. Jan. 1952, pp.14-15.)

May you have the privilege, in a few short years, of kneeling at the altar in the temple. With heads bowed and hands clasped may you experience the fulfillment of your soul's desire to be whole and complete—to function in the full power and glory of your womanhood and manhood.

This Is Forever!

And then when you have spoken your "I do's" may you raise your eyes to each other and look into each other's souls and see there the love which no poet could describe. May you experience an assurance from God the Father that you have been accepted by him. May your souls fill with the unspeakable joy that comes to all who dedicate themselves to God and to each other.

This . . . is Temple Marriage!

Index